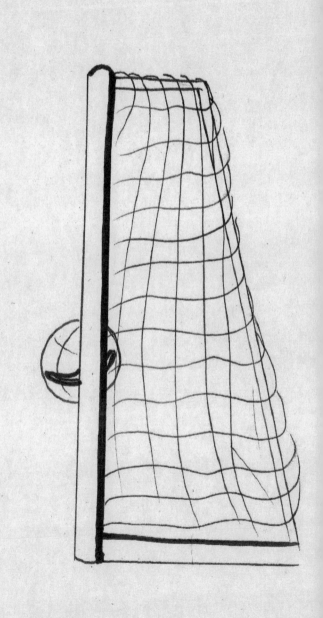

100 FACTS

Spurs

First published in Great Britain in 2016
by Wymer Publishing
www.wymerpublishing.co.uk
Wymer Publishing is a trading name of Wymer (UK) Ltd

First edition. Copyright © 2016 Steve Horton / Wymer Publishing.

ISBN 978-1-908724-18-2

Edited by Jerry Bloom.

Typeset by Andy Francis.
Printed and bound by Clays, Bungay, Suffolk

A catalogue record for this book is available from the British Library.

Cover design by Wymer.
Sketches by Becky Welton. © 2014.

100 FACTS

Spurs

Steve Horton

WP
WYMER
PUBLISHING
Bedford, England

1882
HOTSPUR FC

The club that we now know as Tottenham Hotspur was formed on 5th September 1882 by a group of teenagers who attended bible class at All Hallows Church in Church Lane, Tottenham.

On that day the boys, who were already members of the Hotspur cricket club, paid their first weekly subscriptions. They had already played a game against a side called Radicals a week earlier.

It is believed that the Hotspur name came from the 14th Century nobleman Henry 'Hotspur' Percy, who was depicted in some of William Shakespeare's plays and whose descendants owned land locally.

Friendly games were played on Tottenham Marshes and the first club colours were navy blue. The following year the vicar from All Hallows, John Ripsher, came on board to give the club more organisation. In 1884 the name Tottenham Hotspur was adopted to avoid confusion with another club in South London.

Ripsher remained president of the club until 1894 when he moved to Dover, where he died in poverty in 1907 and was buried in a pauper's grave. One hundred years after his death, a gravestone was placed there after funding was provided by the Tottenham Tribute Trust.

1885
THE FIRST
COMPETITIVE MATCH

Three years after their formation Tottenham Hotspur played their first competitive game in 1885 when they entered the London Association Challenge Cup for the first time.

Tottenham were drawn at home to St Albans in the first round of the competition. There were no reports of the game which took place on 17th October, save for the fact that Tottenham won 5-2. Spurs wore blue and white halved shirts, having been inspired by Blackburn Rovers who they had watched in the previous season's FA Cup final.

In the next round Tottenham were drawn away to Casuals, a team made up of players who were old boys from the public schools. The game was played in Wandsworth and unfortunately Spurs were no match their opponents and were hammered 8-0.

The following year Tottenham entered the competition again but were beaten 6-1 in the first round by Upton Park (who have no connection to West Ham United). In 1887 they lost 6-0 at Hendon in the opening round then in 1888 they were hammered 8-2 at home by Old Etonians, twice winners of the FA Cup. It would not be until fifteen years after their formation that Spurs reached their first cup final.

Tottenham's first game against Arsenal in 1887 was abandoned fifteen minutes before full time due to bad light.

At that time Arsenal were not based in North London, but south of the river in Plumstead and were known as Royal Arsenal. They had only been formed the previous year by workers in a munitions factory.

A friendly game was arranged between the clubs to be played at Tottenham Marshes on 19th November 1887. It was Tottenham's fourth game of the season and they had won the other three comfortably.

Arsenal took the lead after ten minutes and then adopted a defensive approach, but Spurs found a way through and went 2-1 ahead. The only known match report which appeared in the *Weekly Herald* states that they would have scored many more had it not been for the splendid play of Arsenal's keeper.

The report goes on to say that the game, which had started late due to Arsenal's arrival being delayed, had to be stopped fifteen minutes from time "through darkness". Over the next nine years the clubs played seven more friendlies, with Spurs winning four.

1888
NORTHUMBERLAND PARK

Tottenham moved to a new enclosed ground at Northumberland Park in 1888, allowing them to charge admission for the first time.

When home games were played at Tottenham Marshes, the club had no exclusive use of a pitch. Often fights would break out between players of teams to determine who could use the pitches which were in the best condition.

With crowds for Spurs games approaching four figures and being difficult to control, club officials began to look for a more suitable ground. An enclosed plot was found at Northumberland Park, allowing the club to charge admission to games, which was set at three pence.

The first match at the new ground was between Tottenham's reserve side and Stratford St John's, attracting eighty paying spectators. The first proper stand was not built until 1894 and collapsed the following year. There was another unfortunate incident in April 1899 when the roof of a refreshment stall collapsed, causing a number of minor injuries.

By the end of the 19th Century Spurs had turned professional and outgrown Northumberland Park, so moved to White Hart Lane.

1890
RED SHIRTS

In a move that would be unthinkable today, Tottenham changed their kit to red in 1890.

The club had played in blue shirts for three years before changing to blue and white halves in 1885 as a tribute to Blackburn Rovers. After a brief return to blue, in 1890 they switched to red shirts with blue shorts and stockings.

The shirts were made of much heavier material than today and were always long sleeved, with some buttons below the neck. Stockings were worn as opposed to socks as in those days none of the flesh on the players legs was exposed.

Spurs played in these colours for five seasons before switching to an unusual brown and gold stripes, retaining the blue shorts and stockings. In 1898 they returned to a more conventional colour, playing in white shirts, blue shorts and blue stockings. These were taken from Preston North End, one of England's strongest sides at the time.

From the early 1900s more conventional socks were worn and the club have worn the same colours ever since, save for the occasional season in all white.

1892
THE SOUTHERN ALLIANCE

Tottenham played in organised league competition for the first time in 1892-93 when they were a member of the short lived Southern Alliance.

All of the clubs in the two divisions of the Football League were northern and paid their players. In the south though all clubs were amateur with the exception of Arsenal, then known as Woolwich Arsenal.

To increase competition the Southern Alliance was formed and was made up of seven of the strongest amateur teams. As well as Spurs there were Erith, Old St Stephen's, Polytechnic, Slough Town, Upton Park and Windsor & Eton.

Tottenham got off to a good start, winning their first four games, but then won only one of the next four. They ended the season in third place and were the only team to defeat competition winners St Stephen's. Not all fixtures were completed however, and had Polytechnic won all of their outstanding games they would have overhauled Spurs.

The Southern Alliance folded after just one season and it would be three more years before Tottenham were back in organised competition. Of the seven sides who took part, only Slough and Polytechnic survive today.

1894
ENTERING
THE FA CUP

Tottenham entered the FA Cup for the first time in 1894-95 and made it through three qualifying rounds.

In the first qualifying round Spurs were drawn at home against West Hertfordshire, a club that later merged to form Watford. Peter Hunter scored the club's first FA Cup goal and Don Goodall added another before half time, with the *Weekly Herald* reporting that the home side had enjoyed four fifths of the possession.

In the second half Spurs were playing down the slope and were expected to add to their tally but West Herts struck back twice to draw level. Late in the game Goodall restored Tottenham's lead and they had a let off when an opposition shot appeared to bounce over the line after hitting the bar but the referee didn't spot it.

Spurs were drawn at home in the next two qualifying rounds, beating Wolverton 5-3 and Clapton 4-0 in games which both Hunter and Goodall again scored.

In the fourth qualifying round Spurs faced Luton Town, drawing 2-3 at Northumberland Park and then losing the replay 4-0 four days later.

1896
THE
SOUTHERN LEAGUE

After a failed attempt to join the Football League, Tottenham did get themselves back into organised competition in 1896 when they were elected to the Southern League.

Spurs were one of ten clubs that summer who applied to join the 2nd Division of the Football League but they did not secure enough votes to get one of the three available places. The club then turned their attention to the Southern League, which had been formed two years earlier for both professional and amateur clubs.

The league initially consisted of two divisions of seven teams. It was decided to expand the league for 1896-97 but rather than have new teams start in the second tier, three were allowed to be elected straight into the twelve team top flight.

Spurs were one of the lucky three along with Kent sides Gravesend United and Northfleet. Joining them were Wolverston L&NWR and Sheppey United, who had been promoted from the previous season.

The opening game was on 5th September when Spurs drew 3-3 at Sheppey. They did not disgrace themselves and finished fourth, with the most notable result being a 4-0 victory away at Millwall Athletic. They also drew twice with champions Southampton St Mary's, who went the whole season unbeaten.

1897
A FIRST
CUP FINAL

Tottenham's first cup final was in 1896-97 when they were runners up in the Wellingborough Charity Cup.

The invitation competition was organised by the Mayor of Wellingborough for the benefit of charities in the Northamptonshire town. Spurs were one of a number of clubs from the South East and East Midlands to take part.

In the first round Tottenham beat Gravesend United 3-2 at Northumberland Park, then followed this with a 2-0 win at Wolverton. In the semi-final Spurs were drawn against Rushden who they beat 2-1 at Wellingborough.

On 29th April 1897 Spurs were back at the semi-final venue for the final against the competition hosts Wellingborough Town. Play was made difficult for both sides by the wind and low sun and it was the home team who adapted best to the conditions. They won 2-0 thanks to a goal in each half, much to the delight of their fans who swarmed onto the pitch at the end.

After the Wellingborough captain was presented with the cup he and his teammates were applauded by the Tottenham players, who conceded that the better team had won.

Tottenham appointed their first manager in March 1908 when Frank Brettell was persuaded to move south.

Born in Staffordshire in 1862, Brettell played for Everton but after having his career cut short by a broken leg aged just 24, he became a journalist for the Liverpool Mercury.

Brettell remained involved in the game on an administrative level and in 1896 beat off 100 other applicants to become secretary-manager of Bolton Wanderers who were then in the 1st Division.

In March 1898 Brettell's appointment at Tottenham was something of a coup considering he was dropping two tiers into the Southern League. He was paid a salary of £225 a year and still allowed to undertake work for the press if he wished.

Brettell's arrival had an instant impact on the team and they won five of their remaining six games to finish third in the Southern League. However the following February he left Spurs to take over at newly formed Portsmouth who offered him more money.

After two years at Portsmouth Brettell left and managed Plymouth before quitting football altogether in 1905 and working as a clerk.

1898
JACK JONES,
THE FIRST INTERNATIONAL

The first Tottenham player to represent his country was Welsh international John 'Jack' Jones.

Jones joined Spurs in 1897 from Sheffield United, where he had been limited to just 32 appearances in three years. He had also played in the Football League with Grimsby Town and had made his debut for Wales in 1895.

At Sheffield United Jones had been a versatile player as he generally only played when filling in for others who were injured. At Spurs though he settled into the outside left role, the modern day equivalent of a left winger.

His first appearance for Wales whilst a Spurs player was on 19th February 1898 in a British Championship match against Ireland at Llandudno. Wales lost 1-0 and a month later he was in the side that were beaten 5-2 by Scotland in Motherwell. A miserable tournament came to an end at the end of March when Wales lost 3-0 at home to England in a game played in Wrexham.

Back at Tottenham, Jones remained a regular in the side for seven seasons and was captain of the club for the 1901 FA Cup triumph. After leaving Tottenham he coached in South Africa and Ireland before becoming a pattern maker, dying in a workplace accident after a fall in 1931.

After eleven years at Northumberland Park, Tottenham moved to the ground that became known as White Hart Lane in 1899.

With Tottenham now in the Southern League crowds were increasing and Northumberland Park was struggling to cope. Officials turned their eye to a disused plant nursery 100 yards down the road which was owned by the Charrington brewery. Two mobile stands were moved from Northumberland Park to the site, providing cover for up to 2,500 spectators, with the overall capacity being over 20,000.

The first game was a friendly against 1st Division Notts County on Monday 4th September 1899. Notts weren't at full strength but still took the lead. However Spurs came back to win 4-1, thanks in part to the opposition keeper going off injured. The 5,000 fans generated receipts of £115.

The following Saturday 11,000 were present for the first competitive game at the ground, when Queens Park Rangers were beaten 1-0 in the Southern League.

Tom Smith was the scorer of Tottenham's first league goal at the Lane, although at the time the ground was advertised as being on the High Road. It was only after the First World War that the ground was officially named White Hart Lane, due to that being the name of the nearest railway station.

Tottenham celebrated their first season at White Hart Lane by winning the Southern League title.

Spurs got off to a great start by winning their first five games and lost only twice before Christmas, one of them at closest challengers Southampton.

The prolific forward line scored goals for fun with Pratt being a particular danger by bagging three hat-tricks. Spurs took no time to adapt to their new surroundings at White Hart Lane, where they didn't lose a game all season. There were some big wins including a 7-0 thrashing of Thames Ironworks (who became West Ham United) and 5-1 win over Bristol Rovers.

Going out of the FA Cup at the first stage to Southampton probably helped the cause. The Saints went all the way to the final and league form dipped as a result of this run. Along with Tottenham and Southampton, Portsmouth were the other serious title contender and they beat Spurs on 3rd March.

Following that defeat at Portsmouth, Spurs went on a five game unbeaten run that took them to the brink of the title. On 13th April Spurs had their chance when they faced Southampton at home and they made no mistake, winning 2-0 in front of a huge crowd of 15,000.

1901
NON LEAGUE
FA CUP WINNERS

FACT **14**

Tottenham's first FA Cup triumph came in 1901 while they were still an non-league side.

Spurs beat Football League sides Preston and Bury in the early rounds, then knocked out fellow Southern League members Reading in the quarter-final. In the semi-final they were paired with 1st Division West Bromwich Albion, hammering them 4-0 at Villa Park.

Sheffield United were the opponents for the final and a huge crowd of 110,820 attended the final at Crystal Palace. Spurs came from a goal down to lead 2-1, both goals coming from Sandy Brown who became the first player to score in every round of the FA Cup. However Walter Bennett equalised for United meaning a replay was necessary.

The replay took place at Burnden Park, Bolton and attracted only 20,470 spectators. Fred Priest gave United a half-time lead but early in the second half John Cameron equalised. Tom Smith then put Spurs ahead and Brown confirmed victory with three minutes remaining.

Spurs had become the first non-league team to win the FA Cup since the Football League had been formed in 1888. No club has ever managed to repeat the feat of winning the competition while playing outside the top two divisions.

In 1902-03 Tottenham were in the unusual position of having two players in the team with the same name, leading to one changing his to that of his previous club.

In the summer of 1902 Tottenham signed John 'Jack' Jones from fellow Southern League club Bristol Rovers. There was an immediate problem with the club's captain also called John 'Jack' Jones.

Although both players had different middle names, the new signing instead opted to be known as Bristol Jones. Over the next two seasons he scored 35 goals in 58 appearances in all competitions.

In 1903-04 Jones was Tottenham's leading scorer in the Southern League. His fifteen goals included a hat-trick on the last day of the season in a 3-3 raw at Wellingborough. He also scored the only goal in an FA Cup giant killing act when 1st Division Aston Villa were beaten 1-0 at Villa Park.

The 1904-05 season began on 3rd September but shortly before this he contracted typhoid fever. He died on 13th September at the age of just 29. He was described by the *London Daily News* as 'Tottenham's most serviceable forward', the paper adding that he would be greatly missed.

1906
BRITISH BASEBALL
CUP WINNERS

In the early 20th century Tottenham also ran a baseball team, winning the British Cup in 1906.

The sport was played in the summer months and some of the footballers were also part of the baseball team. Spurs were one of six London clubs who set the competition up, the others being Clapton Orient, Fulham, Leyton, Nondescripts and Woolwich Arsenal.

In the league Spurs and Woolwich Arsenal tied for first place. The two clubs then met the week after the season ended in the semi-final of what was dubbed the British Cup, even though only London clubs took part. Spurs won through to the final in which the opponents would be Nondescripts, who had finished bottom of the league.

The final was played at White Hart Lane but didn't capture the public imagination, with just 2,500 spectators attending. The third innings was dominated by Spurs, who got six runs and they eventually won 16-5. The cup was presented by Derby based industrialist Sir Francis Ley, who had introduced the sport to the country after visiting the United States in 1889.

In 1908 Spurs won the cup again, beating Leyton Orient 6-5 in the final in front of just 500 fans at the Clapton Stadium.

1908
ELECTED TO THE
FOOTBALL LEAGUE

When Tottenham gained election to the Football League in 1908 it was after a closely fought contest with Lincoln City.

After Stoke resigned from the 2nd Division applications were sought to fill the vacant place. Spurs were one of five clubs to apply, the others being Lincoln, Rotherham Town, Southport Central and a reconstituted Stoke club.

At the Football League Annual General Meeting in Manchester on 29th June representations were made for each club by their officials before a vote was taken by the league's forty members. Tottenham and Lincoln received seventeen votes each, with Stoke getting six, meaning a run-off had to take place.

The second vote couldn't split the two clubs, with each getting twenty votes. This meant the matter had to be referred to the eight member management committee, who voted 5-3 in favour of Tottenham.

The first Football League game for Spurs was on 1st September 1908 when they beat FA Cup holders Wolverhampton Wanderers 3-0 at White Hart Lane. The first league goal was scored by Vivian Woodward after just six minutes when he pounced on the rebound after the keeper had parried a free kick.

1909
PROMOTION AT THE
FIRST ATTEMPT

Tottenham's inaugural season in the Football League saw them win promotion to the 1st Division.

After beating Wolves in their opening game, Tottenham's form was mixed and although they remained unbeaten at White Hart Lane, they didn't win away from home until a 2-0 victory at Gainsborough Trinity on 21st November.

The win at Gainsborough was the second of six straight wins that lifted them into the top two. In the New Year Spurs went eight games unbeaten and by the middle of March they were top of the table. By now the promotion race had turned into a three way battle between Spurs, West Bromwich Albion and Bolton Wanderers. The unbeaten run was ended with their first defeat of the season, a crucial home loss to Albion.

The race went down to the wire and after Albion completed their fixtures first they were a point ahead of Spurs and Bolton who still had one game each to play.

On 28th April Spurs travelled to Derby knowing that a draw would be enough to go up as they had the better goal average. A second half equaliser from Bobby Steel earned a 1-1 draw and Spurs became the first team to go up at the first attempt since Liverpool in 1894.

1910
THE COCKEREL
AND BALL

The cockerel and ball, a famous feature of Tottenham's White Hart Lane stadium, was added to the West Stand in 1910.

The origin of the cockerel may well go back to Harry Hotspur who reared cockerels for fighting, but the link has never been explained with certainty. The earliest known crest in the 19th Century was a simple spur and at some point a link was made with a cockerel.

Late in 1909 former player W J Scott cast a cockerel and ball in copper which was then perched on top of the new West Stand in 1910. In 1934 the nine foot sculpture was taken down and given a clean then in 1958 the upgrade of floodlights meant it had to be re-sited on the East Stand.

When the stand was renovated in 1989 club officials took the opportunity to investigate rumours that secret club documents had been encased in the ball. A small section was cut away, but all that was found inside was an old club handbook.

The original cockerel now stands in the club reception, with replicas adorning the roofs of both east and west stands.

1912
FACING ARSENAL
IN VIENNA

In the summer of 1912 Tottenham undertook a tour of central Europe where they faced their future rivals in Austria.

Woolwich Arsenal were still a year away from their move to North London. However there was still something of a rivalry as they were the only two clubs from London in the 1st Division.

Spurs began their tour in Belgium where they lost 2-0 to Hull City in Brussels. They then moved on to Germany where they beat VFB Leipzig 3-1.

From Germany it was on to the Austrian capital of Vienna where they enjoyed a good 5-2 win over Wiener SK. However four days later they came unstuck against Woolwich Arsenal, losing 4-0 in a game that had a silver cup and medals on offer for the winners.

Spurs went on to Hungary where they beat champions Ferencvaros 4-1 before playing two games against the Hungarian national side who were preparing for the Olympics. The first game ended in a 2-2 draw and the second was a seven goal thriller, Spurs edging it 4-3.

The final game of the tour saw Tottenham return to Austria where they faced the Austrian Olympic team in Vienna, losing 3-0.

1919
SICK AS
A PARROT

When the Football League resumed after the First World War, Spurs were unexpectedly relegated by Arsenal, an event that may be behind the phrase 'sick as a parrot'.

National football competition was suspended after the 1914-15 season, when Spurs finished bottom of the league. When it was decided to expand the top flight to 22 clubs for 1919-20 it was assumed Spurs and Chelsea would be reprieved from relegation but it didn't work out that way.

League officials decided that Chelsea would be reprieved from relegation but Spurs would have to stand for re-election against the teams who had

finished between third and eighth in the 2nd Division in 1914-15.

Arsenal's chairman Sir Henry Norris argued that they should be elected to the 1st Division due to their long league history. This was then surprisingly backed by John McKenna, the president of the Football League.

Despite having only finished sixth in 1915, Arsenal got eighteen votes to Tottenham's eight. Arguably this is when the great rivalry between the two clubs began.

In a further twist Tottenham's mascot, a parrot given to them by a ship's captain on their return from a tour in South America in 1909, died the same day. This is one of the theories put forward for the reason behind the phrase 'sick as a parrot'.

1920
PROMOTED WITH
RECORD POINTS HAUL

After being denied a place in the expanded top flight, Tottenham took their anger out on the pitch in 1919-20, setting a points record as they romped to promotion.

Tottenham got off to a great start, winning their first seven games and scoring 28 goals. This included a 5-0 win at Coventry and 6-1 home victory over Lincoln. By the time they lost their first game on 8th November, Spurs were five points ahead of third placed Birmingham with thirteen games played.

Over Christmas Tottenham won all three games, including two against fellow challengers Hull City, stretching their advantage over third place to eight points. By the end of March the gap was ten points with White Hart Lane being a fortress, Spurs having won fourteen and drawn one of their fifteen games there.

Promotion was secured on Easter Monday with a 3-1 win at Wolves, meaning promotion had been clinched with five games still to play. A 3-1 win at Stoke in their next game secured the title and by the end of the season Spurs had seventy points, won 32 of their 42 games and scored 102 goals. Under the old two points for a win system, no team in the top two divisions has ever matched Tottenham's record.

1921
KING WATCHES
FA CUP WIN

Spurs won their second FA Cup in 1920-21 and were presented with the trophy by the King.

In the early rounds Tottenham were in devastating form, beating Bristol Rovers 6-2, Bradford City 4-0 and Southend United 4-1. In the quarter-finals they beat Aston Villa 1-0 and then overcame Preston 2-1 in the semi-final in Sheffield.

The final against Wolverhampton Wanderers took place at Chelsea's Stamford Bridge ground. The guest of honour was King George V, only the second time a reigning monarch had attended an

FA Cup final.

The game was played on a boggy pitch and both teams struggled to adapt in the first half, with players often losing their footing. Spurs had the better of the play and tested Wolves' keeper Noel George on a number of occasions.

In the 53rd minute though Wolves' keeper Noel George was finally beaten by Jimmy Dimmock who shook off his marker and scored with a low drive. Tottenham continued to dominate and could have had more. Wolves only threatened in the closing stages but Spurs held on to be worthy winners. The cup and medals were then presented to their players by the King.

1922
THE FIRST
TITLE CHALLENGE

Tottenham had their first serious hopes of winning the 1st Division Championship in 1921-22 but they were unable to overhaul Liverpool.

There was nothing in the first month of the season to indicate that Tottenham would be title contenders as they lost three of their first seven games. They then failed to win during October and were down in eighteenth place at the end of that month.

Over Christmas Spurs finally got going, winning four games in succession to take them up to fifth in the table, but still seven points behind pacesetters Liverpool and Burnley.

A three month spell between January and March when Spurs lost only once lifted them to third, but Liverpool were still eight points clear at the top. However Liverpool drew one and lost one while three straight wins for Spurs, including a 2-0 home victory over Arsenal, narrowed the gap to five points with four games remaining.

With Liverpool having two difficult games against third place Burnley to play, there were hopes Spurs could sneak the title. However they then lost 1-0 at relegation threatened Oldham on Easter Monday. On the same day Liverpool beat Burnley to ensure they couldn't be caught, ending Spurs hopes of becoming champions for the first time.

1925
RESERVES BEAT
REAL MADRID

Tottenham's first encounter with Real Madrid in 1925 was a low key one, with the future Spanish giants facing a Spurs reserve side.

Back in the 1920s Real Madrid were regarded as one of the best teams in Spain. However football in the country was nowhere near as advanced as in England and there wasn't even a national league. Their European tour of 1925 included three games in England and they suffered defeats at Newcastle and Birmingham before arriving in London.

The game against Tottenham's reserves at White Hart Lane on 3rd September 1925 was billed as a match against the 'Royal Sporting Club of Madrid'. In front of the watching Spanish ambassador they played 'good clean football' according to the press, but they lacked in 'quickness and ball control'.

Two goals from Jimmy Townley and one each from Charlie Handley and Knott put Spurs 4-0 up before Martinez pulled two back for the visitors. Madrid's keeper was described as being too short in the press, who also claimed Spurs had enough 'spare energy to make the result more emphatic if they desired'.

The next time Tottenham faced Real Madrid, they were a different proposition altogether and arguably the biggest club in the world.

1925
FRANK OSBORNE'S
HAT TRICK OF HAT TRICKS

Spurs' striker Frank Osborne had a sensational scoring streak in the autumn of 1925 when he scored a hat-trick in three successive games.

Osborne had joined Spurs from Fulham in January 1924 but scored only one goal prior to the start of 1925-26. However he struck up a great understanding with Jimmy Dimmock and Jack Elkes and had scored five times in the opening twelve games of the season. Osborne's prolific spell began against Liverpool at White Hart Lane on 24th October 1925. After scoring with a first half header Liverpool equalised but late in the game he scored two fine individual goals to help Spurs to a 3-1 win.

The following week at Leicester, Tottenham had some desperate bad luck when two players had to go off injured early on. It meant they had to play with nine men as there were no substitutes then. A brave performance saw them go down 5-3, Osborne getting all three of Spurs' goals.

Osborne's remarkable treble was completed the following week when West Ham were the visitors to White Hart Lane. Spurs were 4-0 up within 24 minutes, Osborne scoring the first, second and fourth goals. The game ended 4-2 with Osborne's achievement only being matched by Liverpool's Jack Balmer in 1946.

The first Tottenham manager to bring a prolonged period of success to the club left in 1927 after fifteen years in charge.

For Tottenham's first four years in the Football League, directors oversaw team affairs. However no wins in the first thirteen matches of 1912-13 led to the appointment of former Scotland captain Peter McWilliam.

Tottenham were bottom of the 1st Division when McWilliam joined but he steered the club to safety, winning more games than they lost. After the shock relegation at the Football League Annual General Meeting of 1919 he achieved promotion straight away with a record points haul, then won the FA Cup in 1921.

In 1921-22 Spurs finished second in the league, the highest position attained by a London club and also reached the semi-finals of the FA Cup. McWilliam continued producing good quality sides by nurturing youngsters, but when Middlesbrough offered him almost double his salary, Tottenham's directors refused his request for an increase and he resigned.

McWilliam won promotion with Middlesbrough and was back at Spurs in 1938. However national competitive football was suspended the following year due to the Second World War and he left in 1942. He had though brought one player into the club during 1938-39 that would become a legendary figure; future Double winning manager Bill Nicholson.

THE CRUELEST
OF RELEGATIONS

FACT 28

When Spurs were relegated in 1927-28 their demise was hard to take. They had been challenging for the title in mid season but eventually watched helplessly as one by one their rivals overhauled them.

At Christmas nobody could have foreseen what was to come. Spurs were unbeaten in nine games and in sixth place, six points behind leaders Everton. However they slowly dropped down the table and after picking up just one point from their last four games, they were in seventeenth place when their fixtures were completed on 28th April.

Spurs were now just two points off the bottom and all five teams below them had one or two games left to play. Sheffield United were the first to overhaul them on 30th April, meaning that on 5th May Spurs fans were praying that any two of Sheffield Wednesday, Manchester United, Middlesbrough and Sunderland lost. Draws were no good to Spurs as they had a worse goal average than all of them.

Sunderland won 3-0 at Middlesbrough, condemning their opponents to relegation. There was devastating news from elsewhere though for Spurs fans, as Wednesday beat Aston Villa 2-0 and Manchester United thrashed Liverpool 6-1. Spurs had been relegated having finished in 21th place, one point behind the seven sides above them who were separated by goal average.

TED HARPER'S 36 GOALS
IN 30 GAMES

FACT **29**

Spurs striker Ted Harper had a sensational season in 1930-31 when he scored 36 goals from just thirty games.

Harper was no stranger to extraordinary goalscoring feats, having set a Football League record in 1925-26 when he scored 43 goals for Blackburn Rovers. He signed for Tottenham from Sheffield Wednesday in 1929 and scored ten goals in his first season. In his second though he was unstoppable as Spurs came close to promotion back to the 1st Division.

Harper began the season by hitting five in a 7-1 win over Reading. In the next game he got two as Burnley were beaten 8-1. Before Christmas he got further hat-tricks against Charlton and Port Vale, both of whom were beaten 5-0 at White Hart Lane.

He continued his scoring run in the New Year, scoring in five successive games in January and February. At the end of March Spurs were second in the table and destined for promotion, but Harper sustained a knee injury that kept him out for six games, none of which were won.

By the time Harper returned for the penultimate game West Bromwich Albion had overhauled Spurs and although he scored twice in a 4-2 win over Barnsley, it wasn't enough. His goalscoring hadn't gone unnoticed though and that summer Preston bought him for £5,000.

THE SHELF

FACT **30**

One of the most famous parts of White Hart Lane came into being in 1934 when the East Stand was constructed.

The new stand, designed by Archibald Leitch, was an extension of the 8,000 capacity East Terrace. It could seat 5,100 people and had a gable on the roof to accommodate the press.

Linking the original terrace, which remained uncovered, and the new stand was a middle level of terracing which offered protection from the elements. This had room for 11,000 fans and became known as the Shelf.

Overall the ground capacity was now around 80,000 and the new stand officially opened prior to a game against Aston Villa on 22nd September, which Spurs lost 2-0.

The Shelf offered a great view and became the home of the most vociferous of Tottenham's supporters, who could create a huge amount of noise due to the low roof of the upper tier.

When the East Stand was renovated in 1989 executive boxes were added, taking away part of the Shelf. This reduced its capacity to just 3,000 lucky season ticket holders. That would only last five years though due to government legislation requiring all top flight grounds to become all seater by 1994.

1935
RECORD WINLESS
SEQUENCE

Tottenham's worst sequence of results came in 1934-35 when a run of sixteen games without a win helped condemn them to relegation from the 1st Division.

A 2-1 home win over Grimsby on Boxing Day 1934 left Spurs thirteenth in the table, although they were still only four points off the relegation places. They then went on a disastrous sequence of results that left them marooned at the bottom of the table.

There were heavy defeats at Everton, who won 5-2, and Wolves who beat them 6-2. Spurs had sank into the bottom two by the end of February and then suffered a humiliating 6-0 defeat at home to Arsenal.

On 23rd March Tottenham had a chance to climb out of the relegation zone when they faced twentieth place Middlesbrough away from home, but were beaten 3-1. The next game was against bottom side Leicester, whose 6-0 win meant they climbed above Spurs.

The poor run finally came to an end on Good Friday, 19th April with a 1-0 win over Blackburn at White Hart Lane.

The following day however a 4-1 defeat at Stoke virtually sealed their fate with two games remaining. Spurs goal average was so bad they needed a freak set of results to stay up and unsurprisingly it didn't happen.

One of the greatest FA Cup comebacks of all time saw Spurs come from 3-1 down with just a few minutes remaining to defeat Everton in a 5th round replay.

On 20th February 1937 the two sides drew 1-1 at Goodison Park. Jimmy McConville looked to have put Spurs in the next round but Everton equalised just two minutes from time, setting up a replay at White Hart Lane two days later.

Everton took a 2-0 lead within twenty minutes, their goals coming from Tommy Lawton and Dixie Dean thanks to crosses that had been supplied by Albert Geldard. Johnny Morrison pulled a goal back for Tottenham after half an hour but soon after the restart Dean restored Everton's two goal advantage.

With seven minutes remaining Everton looked to have been awarded a penalty but the referee changed his mind after the linesman told him the ball had gone out of play in the build-up.

A minute after this incident Morrison pulled a goal back and with two minutes left to play Joe Meek scored an equaliser with a stunning solo effort. Morrison then completed his hat-trick before full time to complete a remarkable turnaround. There would be no more joy in the next round though, as Preston won 2-1 at White Hart Lane.

1938
WHITE HART LANE'S
RECORD CROWD

The biggest crowd to attend a match at White Hart Lane is 75,038 for a cup tie when Spurs were in the 2nd Division.

Tottenham beat Blackburn, New Brighton and Chesterfield to reach the quarter-finals of the FA Cup, where they were drawn at home to holders Sunderland.

There were long queues outside the ground on the day of the game and it was soon apparent that the previous record crowd of 71,900 would be beaten. All of the gates were closed fifteen minutes before kick-off with an estimated 10,000 still locked outside. Due to the level of the crushing, several hundred fans were helped over the barriers by police and distributed to other parts of the ground.

The tie looked to be heading for a replay until ten minutes from time when Sunderland scored thanks to a goal by Raich Carter. Spurs tried desperately to equalise and looked like they would when Johnny Morrison's header was goalbound, only for John Mapson's outstretched arm to clear the ball off the line.

The attendance of 75,038 was never bettered. However with Tottenham scheduled to play their Champions League home games at Wembley for 2016-17, there is a very good chance the record will be broken.

In 1938-39 Spurs had a major influence on the decision of football authorities to allow players to wear numbers on the back of their shirts.

Back in 1928 both Arsenal and Chelsea had experimented with the idea in 1st Division games but the Football League banned any further use. Numbers were then used in the 1933 FA Cup final but again the concept didn't continue and the following year the Football League management committee dismissed the idea.

By the end of the decade shirt numbers were back on the agenda and Tottenham were given special permission from the Football Association to wear numbered shirts for their FA Cup third round tie with Watford. On Tuesday 3rd January the press were invited to White Hart Lane to take photographs of the players holding the shirts, numbered simply 1 to 11.

The conditions for the match the following Saturday were treacherous but this didn't do Spurs any harm as they romped to a 7-1 victory. The pitch was so muddy though that it was hard to make out the shirt numbers at the end as they were so filthy.

During the summer the Football League finally allowed the general use of shirt numbering, but the outbreak of the Second World War meant they weren't a regular feature until 1946-47.

1950
BEST SUPPORTED
TEAM PROMOTED

FACT **35**

When Spurs were promoted in 1949-50 they were the best supported team in English football.

Spurs opened the season with two 4-1 victories over Brentford and Plymouth but then lost 3-2 at home to Blackburn. However they then remained unbeaten until the new year, winning eighteen and drawing four of their next 22 games. This gave them a massive thirteen point lead over third place Hull City.

Eight of their crowds during this run were over 50,000 and there was one of 60,000+, against London rivals Queens Park Rangers. Spurs did lose two of their next four games but when fellow challengers Southampton visited White Hart Lane on 25th February, a massive crowd of 70,302 attended.

Promotion was clinched on Good Friday, 7th April 1950. A crowd of 66,889 saw a 0-0 draw with Hull that meant third place Sheffield Wednesday, who were fifteen points behind Spurs with seven games left, couldn't overhaul them.

Tottenham won only one of their last six games but it didn't matter. They still finished nine points clear at the top and their average attendance of 54,111 was more than anyone in the 1st Division, where no team averaged more than 50,000.

1951
1ST DIVISION
CHAMPIONS

Just a year after securing promotion Spurs won their first league title in 1950-51 with a style of football known as 'push and run'.

Spurs lost 4-1 at home to Blackpool in their first top flight game since 1935 but they didn't lose at White Hart Lane again that season. After eight games they were down in twelfth place but by the end of November they had climbed to second, three points behind Arsenal.

Tottenham first went top of the league in the last game of 1950, when Charlton were beaten 1-0 at White Hart Lane. Going out of the FA Cup in the 3rd round may then have been helpful as it allowed them to concentrate on the league.

Nobody could deal with the 'push and run' style the players had been coached by manager Arthur Rowe. This involved using the modern day one-two to maximum effect, with attackers running forward to collect a return pass before defenders knew what was happening. In the days of 2-3-5 formations, it was highly effective.

The title was clinched in the penultimate game, when a Len Duquemin goal was enough to beat Sheffield Wednesday. Spurs finished four points ahead of Manchester United and became the third team to be champions of the 2nd and 1st Division in successive seasons.

1953
FLOODLIT FOOTBALL
AT WHITE HART LANE

FACT 37

The first floodlights at White Hart Lane were erected in 1953 and first used for a friendly between Tottenham and Racing Club Paris.

Although the football authorities were still not allowing competitive games to be played under lights the number of clubs installing them for prestige friendlies was increasing. Tottenham's big switch on

took place on 29th September 1953 with a game against Racing Club Paris, who along with Marseille had won the Coupe de France a record five times.

The French side played some skilful football in the first half and deservedly led 1-0 at the break. However the second half, which was broadcast live on television, was a goal fest. Rain had made the pitch slippery and this suited Spurs' fast playing style perfectly. Racing Club couldn't cope and goals from Len Duquemin, Les Bennett (2), George Hutchinson and Ron Burgess gave them a 5-3 victory in front of a crowd of 27,963.

The FA finally allowed games to be played under floodlights in 1956 and the original set at White Hart Lane was replaced in the 1970s.

1954
DANNY
BLANCHFLOWER

In 1954 Tottenham beat off Arsenal to the signature of midfielder Danny Blanchflower, who would become one of the most influential players in the club's history.

The £30,000 that Spurs paid was a huge fee the 28 year old, who had become disillusioned at Aston Villa and knew time was running out if he wanted success. He made his debut on 11th December 1954 at Manchester City in a game that finished 0-0.

Blanchflower's first full season saw a brush with relegation but they then finished second and third. In 1958-59 Bill Nicholson was appointed manager and made Blanchflower captain, having initially dropped him from the team. After avoiding relegation Spurs then went on to finish third the following season, just two points behind champions Burnley.

Despite now being in his mid thirties, Blanchflower showed no sign of slowing down as he led Spurs to the Double in 1960-61 and FA Cup in 1961-62. He was injured for much of 1962-63 and when he did regain his fitness he struggled to cope with the increased physical demands of the game. He announced his retirement in a newspaper column in 1964.

Blanchflower later managed Chelsea and Northern Ireland. He died in 1993 and in 2009 was named as Tottenham's best ever player by *The Times*.

ARTHUR ROWE
LEAVES

FACT 39

Tottenham's first title winning manager was forced to leave the club in 1955 due to ill health.

Arthur Rowe played 201 games for Tottenham in all competitions in the 1930s, also appearing once for England. His playing career was ended by a cartilage injury and after turning Chelmsford into a leading non league side, he took over at White Hart Lane in 1949.

Rowe won promotion in his first season and then led Spurs to their first league championship. A great thinker and innovator, he adopted the "push and run" system that opposition defenders couldn't cope with.

When asked about it by Reg Drury from the *Enfield Gazette*, Rowe replied that it was just a case of doing the obvious and that sometimes players made football too difficult. One of his favourite dressing room phrases to the players was "keep it simple".

After winning the title in 1950-51 Tottenham finished second the following season but then dropped down to tenth and sixteenth. The inability to bring back the glory days took its toll and Rowe had a nervous breakdown. He resigned in 1955 and took a few years out of the game, later having a spell as manager of Leyton Orient.

Tottenham scored 100 goals in 1956-57, but the feat wasn't enough to overhaul Manchester United in the table.

Spurs started as they meant to go on, winning 4-1 at Preston on the opening day of the season. Their first home game saw Manchester City beaten 5-1 and a run of six straight wins in September and October brought return of 24 goals.

The goals were spread along the forward line, with Terry Medwin, Tommy Harmer and Alf Stokes all getting their fair share. There wasn't a game at White Hart Lane where Spurs didn't score and they only failed to find the net four times on their travels.

Big home wins were 6-0

over Everton, 6-2 against Charlton and 5-0 against both Cardiff and Luton. Away from home, Spurs struck four against Chelsea and Aston Villa in addition to their opening day haul at Preston. They were rampant in the FA Cup too, winning 4-0 against Chelsea while on a past season tour to America Manitoba All Stars were hammered 12-0.

Despite ending the season with 104 goals in the league, they finished eight points behind champions Manchester United, whose team were commonly known as the Busby Babes.

Legendary manager Bill Nicholson's first game in charge of Tottenham was a record breaking one. Tottenham beat Everton 10-4 in what remains the highest scoring game in the English top flight.

Spurs were second from bottom in the league and manager Jimmy Anderson had resigned a few days earlier. His replacement was coach Bill Nicholson whose first game as manager could not have been more sensational.

Alf Stokes opened the scoring for Tottenham but Everton equalised through Jimmy Harris. Spurs then took control with two goals from Bobby Smith, one each from Terry Medwin and George Robb and another by Stokes giving them a 6-1 half-time lead.

Early in the second half Harris scored for Everton but Smith then completed his hat-trick and Tommy Harmer made it 8-2. Harris got a hat-trick of his own before Smith added another, putting Spurs 9-3 ahead. Bobby Collins got another back for Everton then Johnny Ryden made it double figures for Spurs and the game ended 10-4.

As Tottenham's players were congratulated by a delighted Nicholson on leaving the field, Harmer joked that they wouldn't win 10-4 every week. It is hard to believe that such a scoreline could occur in the English top division ever again.

1960
RECORD VICTORY

Spurs' record victory came in an FA Cup 4th round replay against 4th Division Crewe Alexandra in 1959-60.

The two sides drew 2-2 in the first game in Crewe, and for the replay thousands of visiting fans who worked on the railways took advantage of free travel to descend on White Hart Lane.

Spurs were 2-0 up within ten minutes thanks to Bobby Smith and Les Allen. Smith then added another before Tim Coleman got one for Crewe. Tommy Harmer made it 4-1 in the twentieth minute and on the half hour Allen got his second.

Smith completed his hat-trick in the 33rd minute and then got another to make it 7-1. Cliff Jones made it 8-1 before Allen scored his third and fourth goals in quick succession. The half-time scoreline was an incredible 10-1 and Smith had also had a goal ruled out for offside.

In the 56th minute Jones scored Spurs' eleventh but there were then 23 goalless minutes until Allen got his fifth and Tottenham's twelfth. A poor clearance then saw Bert Llewellyn score for Crewe and the rout was completed when Roy Warhurst converted a penalty after being brought down in the box.

As well as being Tottenham's record victory, the 13-2 game was also the highest scoring FA Cup tie of the 20th Century.

Spurs began the 1960-61 season with eleven straight wins, a top flight record that still stood at the end of 2015-16.

The season began with a 2-0 win over Everton at White Hart Lane, the goals coming from Bobby Smith and Les Allen. Spurs then won two successive games in Lancashire, 3-1 against Blackpool and 4-1 against Burnley.

Smith scored a hat-trick as Blackpool were beaten 3-1 at White Hart Lane then there was an impressive 4-1 win over Manchester United. Spurs then won 2-1 at Bolton before a hard fought 3-2 derby win over Arsenal at Highbury.

The eighth victory was a 3-1 home win against Bolton then Leicester were beaten 2-1 at Filbert Street. In the next game Aston Villa were thumped 6-2 at White Hart Lane in front of a crowd of 61,356, the biggest of the season so far. Smith scored one of the goals in this game, taking his tally to thirteen.

The eleventh straight win was a 4-0 hammering of Wolves at Molineux. The run finally came to an end on 10th October 1960 when Manchester City drew 1-1 at White Hart Lane.

The winning sequence remains a top flight record from the start of the season, although Manchester United almost matched it in 1985-86 when they won their first ten games.

The 1960-61 season saw Tottenham become the first club of the 20th Century to win the League Championship and FA Cup Double.

After the great eleven game winning start Tottenham were never off the top of the table. They clinched the title on 17th April 1961 when closest challengers Sheffield Wednesday were beaten 2-1 at White Hart Lane. Spurs scored a total of 115 league goals and the leading scorer was Bobby Smith with 28.

In the FA Cup Spurs eliminated Charlton, Crewe, Aston Villa and Sunderland to reach the semi-finals, where they beat Burnley 3-0. Their opponents for the final on 6th May were Leicester, who had won 3-2 at White Hart Lane earlier in the season.

The first half was frustrating for Tottenham who were unable to break down Leicester's defence. However when Len Chalmers broke his leg in the 38th minute it meant Leicester would have to continue the game with ten men.

In the 66th minute Bobby Smith collected a pass from Terry Dyson and fired the ball past Gordon Banks to give Spurs the lead. With nine minutes remaining Smith set up Dyson to score Spurs' second.

Tottenham had become the first team of the 20th Century to win the Double, the last team to achieve it having been Aston Villa in 1897.

1961
TERRY DYSON'S
DERBY HAT-TRICK

The only Tottenham player to score a hat-trick in a North London derby is Terry Dyson in a seven goal thriller at White Hart Lane on 26th August 1961.

Tottenham had begun their title defence with a win at Blackpool and then drew 2-2 at home with West Ham, a game in which Dyson got two goals. Arsenal were the next visitors to White Hart Lane in a game that attracted a crowd of 59,371.

Les Allen opened the scoring for Spurs in the sixteenth minute and five minutes later Dyson doubled the lead, netting the rebound after his header hit the bar. Alan Skirton pulled one back for Arsenal and then in the second half two goals from Mel Charles gave the Gunners the lead.

However Tottenham weren't finished and two goals in as my minutes from Dyson sent the home fans into raptures. The first of these came after the ball had struck his arm and he later admitted that had the referee seen it the goal may have been disallowed. The second and ultimately winning goal came after a brilliant one-two with Danny Blanchflower.

Dyson later played for Fulham and Colchester and published his autobiography, *Spurs' Unsung Hero of the Glory Years*, in 2015.

1962
TWO SEMI FINALS
IN A WEEK

In 1961-62 Tottenham couldn't quite retain the title but they had success in the cups.

Spurs were never able to get over losing three of their first nine games and eventually finished third in the league. In the cups though they were unstoppable and reached the semi-finals of both the European and FA Cups.

In the first leg of the European Cup semi-final Spurs were beaten 3-1 by holders Benfica in Lisbon. Prior to the second leg, they had to play an FA Cup semi-final against Manchester United in Sheffield on 31st March 1962. Tottenham reached Wembley by beating the Red Devils 3-1 thanks to goals from Terry Medwin, Jimmy Greaves and Cliff Jones.

Five days later, on 5th April, 64,448 packed into White Hart Lane to see if Spurs could overturn their European Cup deficit. The task was made almost impossible when Aguas scored in the fifteenth minute, but Bobby Smith scored ten minutes before half-time to give Spurs hope.

Two minutes after the break Danny Blanchflower converted a penalty meaning one more goal would force a replay. Despite relentless pressure which saw Spurs hit the post twice and bar once, they fell just short. Benfica went on to beat Real Madrid 5-3 in the final.

1962
THE CHESSBOARD
FINAL

When Tottenham retained the FA Cup in 1961-62 the press dubbed the game 'The Chessboard Final' due to the cautious tactical approach of both sides.

Tottenham beat Birmingham, Plymouth, West Bromwich Albion, Aston Villa and Manchester United to reach Wembley. Their opponents for the final were Burnley, who had finished second in the league, one place ahead of Spurs.

Jimmy Greaves opened the scoring for Tottenham in the third minute but their were no more goals in the first half. Five minutes after the break Jimmy Robson equalised but Bobby Smith restored Tottenham's lead just a minute later.

Spurs had a major let-off midway through the second half when Robson had a goal ruled out for offside, which television replays later showed was not conclusive. With ten minutes left Spurs were awarded a penalty for a handball on the line and Danny Blanchflower sent the keeper the wrong way to seal the victory.

Although the press dubbed the game the 'Chessboard Final' due to the pace of the game being much slower than previous finals, the statistics show a different picture. There was plenty of play in the penalty areas and there were more shots on target than in any final since the Second World War.

1963
EUROPEAN CUP WINNERS CUP WINNERS

FACT 48

Tottenham became the first British side to win a European trophy in 1963 when they won the European Cup Winners Cup.

Spurs qualified for the competition due to having won the FA Cup in 1961-62. Their first tie was an all British affair against Glasgow Rangers, with Spurs winning 5-2 at White Hart Lane and then 3-2 at Ibrox.

The next round was the quarter-final where Spurs were beaten 2-0 in the first leg by Slovan Bratislava in Czechoslovakia. Back at White Hart Lane they overturned this in some style, winning 6-0. Spurs were drawn against Yugoslav side OFK Belgrade in the semi-final, winning 2-1 away and 3-1 at home. This set up a final with holders Atletico Madrid at the Feyenoord Stadium in Rotterdam.

The Spaniards played a rough game but Spurs kept their cool and Jimmy Greaves volleyed them into the lead in the sixteenth minute. John White added a second ten minutes before half time but two minutes after the break Atletico scored from a penalty after Ron Henry had handballed.

Midway through the second half Spurs went 3-1 up when Terry Dyson's hopeful punt was misjudged by the keeper. Greaves made it 4-1 in the eightieth minute when he converted a Dyson cross and Dyson himself got the fifth with a long range effort.

1964
DEATH OF
JOHN WHITE

Tottenham suffered a tragic loss in the summer of 1964 when midfielder John White was killed after being struck by lightning.

A key member of the Double winning side, as well as that which won the FA Cup and European Cup Winners Cup in subsequent years, White had scored 47 goals in 217 games for Spurs. In addition to his eye for goal he worked hard and had great skill on the ball.

On 21st July 1964 Spurs' players reported for pre-season training in the morning and were free to do what they liked in the afternoon. Despite the gloomy skies White decided to have a game of golf and went alone to the Crews Hill club in Enfield. When the storm began White took shelter under a tree but was struck by a bolt of lightning and died.

Arguably, White's death was the reason behind Tottenham's fall from grace in the 1960s, as along with Danny Blanchflower's impending retirement his death left a huge void in the squad.

White left a widow and two young children, one of which wrote his biography *The Ghost of White Hart Lane*. A plaque is now sited at the hole which he was playing when he took shelter.

1965
THE FIRST
SUBSTITUTE

The first time Tottenham used a substitute in a match was in the North London derby in 1965.

Substitutions were not allowed prior to the 1965-66 season and even then the Football League stated they could only be used to replace injured players.

In Tottenham's sixth game of the season against Arsenal at White Hart Lane on 11th September 1965 winger Derek Possee picked up an injury, leading to him being replaced by Roy Low. The game went on to finish 2-2 with Alan Gilzean and Frank Saul scoring for Spurs after they had been two down at half-time.

Neither Low nor the player he replaced went on to enjoy much of a career at Tottenham. Left winger Low

would play only eight games for the club, scoring once, before leaving for Watford in 1967. He stayed there just one season before drifting out of the professional game altogether.

Low's replacement Possee also left in 1967, having made nineteen appearances. He went on to make a name for himself in the lower leagues with Millwall, Crystal Palace and Leyton Orient.

One of the most memorable games to feature on the BBC's Match of the Day in its earliest years was Tottenham's 5-1 demolition of Manchester United on 16th October 1965.

The famous highlights show had begun the previous season and in those days only one game was featured a week. With Manchester United being the reigning champions and Spurs having won the Double in 1961, this fixture was a natural choice on this particular Saturday.

Tottenham opened the scoring when Alan Gilzean prodded in from close range. Teenager Neil Johnson then scored his first goal for the club and the score remained 2-0 at half-time.

Jimmy Greaves rounded off a great solo run by rounding the keeper to make it 3-0 and Eddie Clayton got the fourth with a long range effort. United then got one back through Bobby Charlton whose shot from outside the box was arguably the best goal of the game.

Jimmy Robertson rounded off the scoring to make it 5-1, a result that lifted Spurs to fourth in the league, three points behind leaders Sheffield United.

Ironically, when the two sides met against at Old Trafford in December, United won 5-1 in a game that was also televised. Spurs eventually finished that season in eighth place.

1967
THE COCKNEY
CUP FINAL

When Tottenham won the FA Cup in 1967 it was the first final to be contested between two London clubs.

Tottenham knocked out Millwall, Portsmouth, Bristol City and Birmingham in the early rounds. They then beat Nottingham Forest 2-1 in the semi-final at Hillsborough to set up a final with Chelsea. It was to the first time two London clubs had met in the final and was dubbed 'The Cockney Cup Final' by the media.

The match failed to live up to expectations with Chelsea's game plan being to snuff out the threat of Jimmy Greaves, who had scored six goals on the road to Wembley. It largely worked but with five minutes of the first half left Alan Mullery's long range shot was blocked into the path of Jimmy Robertson, who scored with a low drive from the edge of the area.

Tottenham remained on top in the second half and Frank Saul added a second in the 67th minute when he turned and scored with a half volley after receiving the ball with his back to goal. Bobby Tambling netted a consolation for Chelsea with five minutes left.

Although it wasn't the most entertaining of games it was Tottenham's third FA Cup success that decade and also maintained their 100% record in finals.

1970
JIMMY GREAVES
LEAVES

Jimmy Greaves, Tottenham's record breaking goalscorer left the club at the end of 1969-70.

The then 21 year old signed from AC Milan in December 1961 for £99,999, a fee agreed to relieve the pressure of him being the first £100,000 player. He had become unsettled in Italy and was allowed to leave after just six months. He chose Spurs ahead of his former club Chelsea, where he scored 127 goals in four seasons.

Greaves scored in the finals of the 1962 FA Cup and 1963 European Cup Winners Cup. He was the 1st Division's top scorer in 1962-63 and 1963-64 and joint top in 1964-65. In 1966-67 he was the leading scorer in the FA Cup, although he failed to find the net when Spurs beat Chelsea in the final.

In 1968-69 Greaves was again the top scorer in the 1st Division but the following season the team struggled and he was dropped after an FA Cup defeat to Crystal Palace. In March 1970 he joined West Ham in part exchange for Martin Peters, but still finished the season as Spurs' joint leading scorer.

Greave's 266 goals in all competitions for Tottenham makes him the club's record scorer. He is also the highest goalscorer in English top flight football and after retiring in 1971 enjoyed a media career.

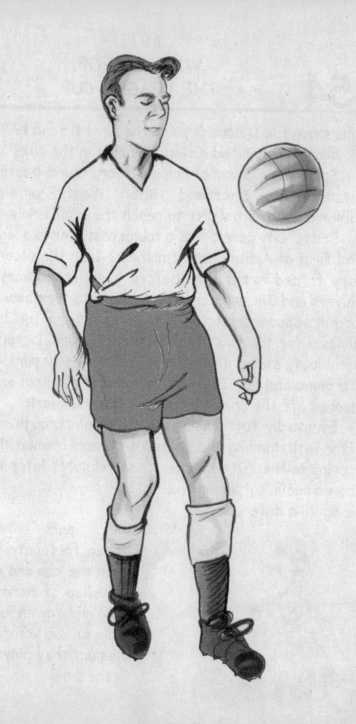

1971
WINNERS OF
THE LEAGUE CUP

FACT **54**

Spurs won the League Cup for the first time in 1970-71, beating a spirited Aston Villa side in the final.

Spurs were drawn at home in every round, beating Swansea City, Sheffield United, West Bromwich Albion and Coventry City to reach the semi-finals.

Bristol City gave Spurs a tough test over two legs. The first at Ashton Gate finished 1-1. In the second they forced extra time before goals from Martin Chivers and Jimmy Pearce took Spurs to Wembley.

Final opponents Aston Villa were playing in the 3rd Division for the first time in their history. Despite their lowly status they dominated the early part of the game and Pat Jennings was grateful a shot was cleared off the line. Another hit the woodwork.

Eventually Tottenham's quality shone through and after withstanding the pressure Chivers opened the scoring in the 79th minute. Three minutes later he scored again, outpacing the tiring Villa defenders.

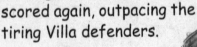

Spurs had been fortunate to win the cup and on the lap of honour Villa were given just as big an ovation for the part they played in the final.

Spurs won the 1971-72 UEFA Cup, beating Wolves in the first all English European final.

Spurs progressed comfortably in the 1st round, beating Icelandic side Keflavik 6-1 away and 9-0 at home. They then had a narrow 1-0 aggregate win over Nantes before beating Romanian side Rapid Bucharest 5-0 over two legs.

In the quarter-final they faced Romanian opposition again, winning 2-0 away to UT Arad then drawing 1-1 at White Hart Lane. They then edged past AC Milan in the semi-final, coming from behind to win 2-1 at home then drawing 1-1 in the San Siro, Alan Mullery getting the vital away goal.

The final was over two legs. In the first at Molineux Martin Chivers gave Spurs the lead shortly before the hour. Wolves equalised but Spurs regained the advantage with a stunning 25 yard drive from Chivers three minutes from time.

54,303 crammed into White Hart Lane for the second leg. Mullery headed Spurs into a 1-0 lead after half an hour but Dave Wagstaffe equalised for Wolves before half time. In the second half Spurs attacked rather than sit back on their slender aggregate lead. Spurs were then presented with the new UEFA Cup trophy, the competition having been re-named from the Fairs Cup.

In 1972-73 Spurs became the first club to win the League Cup for a second time, the winning goal coming from substitute Ralph Coates.

Tottenham beat Huddersfield at home in the second round then overcame Middlesbrough in a tie that required two replays. In the fourth round they beat Millwall 2-0 at White Hart Lane and the quarter-final saw Spurs draw 1-1 at Anfield before winning the replay 3-1.

In the semi-final against Wolves, Spurs won 2-1 at Molineux in the first leg. In the second Wolves forced extra time by winning 2-1 after ninety minutes but a goal from Martin Peters took Spurs to Wembley.

The final was against Norwich City, who were enjoying their first season in the top flight. After 25 minutes John Pratt picked up and injury and had to go off, to be replaced by Coates.

The match was not a classic and the deadlock was eventually broken by Coates in the 72nd minute when his low drive from the edge of the area through a crowd of players found the net. Norwich were forced to attack and the closest they came to equalising was when a Duncan Forbes header went just wide.

Spurs had now won a trophy three years running and had become the first club to win the League Cup twice.

1974
BILL NICHOLSON
LEAVES

Tottenham's most successful manager left at the end of 1973-74 after fifteen years in charge.

Bill Nicholson broke into the Tottenham first team in 1938-39 aged nineteen, but his career was then interrupted due to the Second World War. When the Football League resumed in 1946 he became a prominent figure in the Spurs midfield and was part of the 'push and run' team that won the championship in 1950-51.

After retiring from playing in 1955 Nicholson coached at the club and was appointed team manager in 1958. He led Spurs to the Double in 1961, the FA Cup in 1962 then European Cup Winners Cup in 1963. There was further FA Cup success in 1967 along with another European trophy, the UEFA Cup in 1972. He also oversaw two League Cup triumphs.

Nicholson was a perfectionist who believed in hard work and dedication to the club by all, regardless of status. As the 1970s dawned though, he became increasingly disillusioned at the increasing in wages for players and would also make jibes about their long hairstyles.

Hooliganism by some Spurs' fans at the 1974 UEFA Cup final in Holland hit Nicholson hard and he resigned in August that year. In 1976 he came back on a consultancy basis and was later club president until his death in 2004.

1975
GLENN HODDLE'S
DEBUT

A teenager who went on to become one of Tottenham's greatest players made his debut on 30th August 1975.

Glenn Hoddle was just seventeen years old when he came on as a substitute in a 2-2 draw with Norwich at White Hart Lane. The following February he started a game for the first time, scoring a spectacular goal in a 2-1 win at Stoke.

The midfield playmaker was in outstanding form as Spurs won promotion back to the top flight at the first attempt in 1977-78. In 1979-80 he got his first England cap and was named PFA Young Player of the Year after scoring nineteen league goals for Tottenham.

Hoddle helped Spurs to the 1980-81 and 1981-82 FA Cup finals, scoring in both the first match and replay in 1982. In September 1983 he scored one of Tottenham's best ever goals away to Watford, turning his defender and then chipping the keeper from the corner of the penalty area. The following month, his performance against Feyenoord in a 6-2 aggregate UEFA Cup win was so good that Dutch legend Johann Cruyff presented Hoddle with his shirt.

Hoddle's last game for Spurs was the 3-2 defeat to Coventry in the 1986-87 FA Cup final. That summer he joined Monaco, having scored 110 goals in 490 games for Spurs.

Spurs avoided the drop in their last game of the 1974-75 season with a Cyril Knowles inspired 4-2 win over Leeds United.

Left back Knowles was famous for his crosses and set prices. He was also the inspiration for a song by The Cockerel Chorus, Nice One Cyril, which reached number fourteen in the charts in 1973.

A 1-0 defeat at Arsenal on the last Saturday of 1974-75 left Spurs in the relegation zone. However they had one game left on the following Monday against Leeds, knowing that victory would ensure safety as fourth bottom Luton had completed their fixtures.

There was a crowd of 49,886 for the crucial game against a side that had reached the European Cup final. Knowles put Spurs ahead after just five minutes with one of his trademark free kicks, but despite dominating they couldn't extend their lead before half-time.

Early in the second half Martin Chivers scored from close range and on the hour Knowles converted a penalty after Steve Perryman was fouled in the box by Trevor Cherry.

Tottenham's fans became nervous when Joe Jordan scored for Leeds but Alfie Conn made it 4-1 leading to wild celebrations. Peter Lorimer scored a late goal for Leeds and at the final whistle fans swarmed on to the pitch to celebrate the survival.

1976
KEITH BURKINSHAW
TAKES OVER

Spurs' most successful manager apart from Joe Nicholson was Keith Burkinshaw, who was appointed in 1976.

As a player Burkinshaw plied his trade in the lower divisions then coached in Zambia and at Newcastle United, joining the Tottenham coaching staff in 1975.

When Terry Neill quit as manager to join Arsenal, where he had once been a player, the Tottenham board opted for continuity and appointed Burkinshaw.

One of the first things Burkinshaw did was persuade Bill Nicholson to return to Spurs as chief scout. Burkinshaw knew Nicholson's ability to pick out players, meaning he could be left to look after coaching and tactics.

In Burkinshaw's first season in charge Spurs were relegated, having finished ninth in 1975-76. However the board retained their faith in him and they were promoted at the first attempt. He went on to lead the club to success in the FA Cup two years running (1981 and 1982) and won the UEFA Cup in 1984.

Despite the UEFA Cup success Burkinshaw left after falling out with the board, telling reporters that 'there used to be a football club in there' when he left White Hart Lane for the last time.

Tottenham's biggest victory margin in a league game came on 22nd October 1977 when debutant Colin Lee hit four in a 9-0 win over Bristol Rovers.

Two days before the game Keith Burkinshaw paid £60,000 to Torquay United for Lee and put him straight into the side. After 21 minutes he opened the scoring, reacting quickest to a goalmouth scramble after a Glenn Hoddle cross.

Four minutes later Lee made it 2-0, heading in a John Pratt corner. Spurs went three up just before half time, Hoddle crossing for Peter Taylor whose header looped over the keeper.

Ian Moores scored from a title angle on 56 minutes to make it 4-0 and Lee completed his hat-trick with fifteen minutes remaining when he again scored with a header from a corner. Moore then scored twice in a minute to get a hat-trick of his own and with two minutes remaining Lee stabbed home his fourth and Tottenham's eighth from the edge of the six yard box.

The rout was completed by Hoddle, whose simple tap in from Moore's cross gave Spurs a nine goal winning margin that has never been repeated in the league. They were promoted back to the 1st Division at the end of the season and have never been out of the top flight since.

In the summer of 1978 newly promoted Tottenham stunned the football world when they signed two World Cup winners.

Players from outside the British Isles were a rarity back then so it was a major shock when Tottenham persuaded two members of Argentina's World Cup winning squad, Osvaldo Ardiles and Ricardo Villa, to join them.

Their debuts were on 19th August 1978 when Villa scored in a 1-1 draw at champions Nottingham Forest. The following week there was a Argentinean style ticker tape reception at White Hart Lane but the game didn't go to plan, Spurs losing 4-1 to Aston Villa.

Ardiles settled in to the English game far better than Villa. For the 1981 FA Cup final the squad song, sung with Chas and Dave, was entitled 'Ossie's Dream' but it would be Villa who was the hero in the final.

Villa left at the end of his contract in 1983, returning to South America but Ardiles stayed until 1988. Although Ardiles went on to play and manage abroad, his home has always been in Hertfordshire and his sons have never lived anywhere else. Ardiles also set a trend in 1993 when he was the first manager from outside the British Isles to be appointed at a Premier League club.

FACT 63
RICKY VILLA'S FA CUP
HEARTBREAK AND GLORY

Ricky Villa fired Tottenham Hotspur to glory in the FA Cup final replay in 1981, having left the pitch in tears during the first game.

With Spurs trailing the 100th final 1-0 to Manchester City a disappointing Villa was substituted in the 68th minute by Keith Burkinshaw and was devastated as he walked off the pitch. An own goal by City's Tommy Hutchinson though earned Spurs a draw and Villa kept his place in the starting eleven for the replay on Thursday 14th May.

Villa put Spurs ahead in the eighth minute but this was soon cancelled out by Steve Mackenzie. Early in the second half City went ahead thanks to a Kevin Reeves penalty but in the 70th minute Garth Crooks equalised for Spurs.

In the 76th minute there seemed little danger when Villa collected a pass from Tony Galvin. However from thirty yards out he went on a weaving run, beating four City defenders before slotting the ball past keeper Joe Corrigan who was trying to close him down.

Villa's goal meant Tottenham had won the FA Cup for the sixth time and it was by far his finest moment at the club. In 2001 it was voted Wembley's goal of the century when the famous old stadium was demolished.

Spurs retained the FA Cup in 1982, equalling the record for the most wins in the competition. The route to the final included wins over London rivals Arsenal and Chelsea, as well as Aston Villa who would become European champions that season. They beat Leicester in the semi-final to set up an all London final with Queens Park Rangers who had narrowly missed out on promotion from the 2nd Division.

The first game saw very little goalmouth action and Spurs were restricted to long shots. There was no score after ninety minutes and there were no goals in the first period of extra time. Glenn Hoddle's deflected shot gave Spurs the lead five minutes into the second period but Terry Fenwick's header forced a replay.

Six minutes into the replay, which took place on 27th May 1982, Graham Roberts was brought down in the area and Hoddle converted the resultant penalty. Spurs were on the backfoot for much of the game and had a scare when John Gregory's chip hit the bar but they held on for victory.

The win meant Tottenham has become the first club to retain the FA Cup since they did so themselves twenty years earlier. It was also their seventh triumph, equalling Aston Villa's record.

FACT 65

Spurs' biggest post-war win in a North London derby came on Easter Monday 1983 when Arsenal were beaten 5-0 at White Hart Lane.

Both sides were playing for pride by this stage of the season, with Tottenham tenth and Arsenal eleventh in the table. Earlier in the season Spurs had lost 2-0 at Highbury and were out for revenge in this return fixture.

Tottenham were without the suspended Steve Perryman while Glenn Hoddle, Ricky Villa and Ossie Ardiles were all injured. Manager Keith Burkinshaw went for an attacking line-up, naming Steve Archibald, Alan Brazil, Mark Falco and Terry Gibson in the starting eleven.

Within eighteen minutes of the kick-off Spurs were leading 3-0. Defender Chris Hughton scored the first and third goals with finishes that strikers would have been proud of, while the second goal was a stunning volley by Brazil.

In the second half Falco got his second after a long ball into the box which the Arsenal defence had completely misjudged. Brazil then seized on another defensive error to poke the ball home and score his first goal for Spurs.

The 5-0 victory was Tottenham's biggest win over Arsenal since they won by the same scoreline on Christmas Day 1911.

Spurs' biggest away win in European competition came against Irish debutants Drogheda United on 14th September 1983.

The 1st round 1st leg of this UEFA Cup tie took place at Drogheda's United Park in front of 7,000 fans. Spurs' opponents had qualified for European competition for the first time by finishing second in the league the previous season. Due to their ground having no floodlights, the game kicked off at 4.30pm.

Mark Falco opened the scoring for Tottenham after just five minutes with Garth Crooks adding another shortly after the half hour. As half-time approached, Tony Galvin's rather tame effort was fumbled by Drogheda's keeper to give Spurs a 3-0 lead at the break.

Gary Mabbutt got Tottenham's fourth after 51 minutes and sixteen minutes from time Falco scored his second to make it 5-0. Mabbutt then completed the scoring with nine minutes to go.

In the second leg Spurs did even better, thrashing Drogheda 8-0 at White Hart Lane in a game where Falco again scored twice. Spurs went on to win the competition that season but it would be 22 years before the Irish side played in Europe again.

The UEFA Cup was won for the second time in 1983-84, beating Anderlecht in a thrilling penalty shoot-out at White Hart Lane.

Tottenham defeated Dutch giants Feyenoord and German heavyweights Bayern Munich on the way to the final where they faced holders Anderlecht of Belgium.

In the first leg in Brussels, Spurs led 1-0 with five minutes left thanks to a Paul Miller goal but Morten Olsen equalised for Anderlecht. At White Hart Lane, the Belgians took the initiative on the hour through Alex Czerniatynski. However with six minutes remaining Graham Roberts got a deserved equaliser for Tottenham.

There were no further goals in extra time so with the sides level on away goals a penalty shoot-out was required. This meant Spurs' number two keeper Tony Parks would have to step up to the mark with regular stopper Ray Clemence being injured.

Roberts scored Spurs' first penalty then Parkes saved Anderlecht's. The next six penalties were scored meaning Danny Thomas would win the cup for Spurs if he converted their fifth penalty. However, it was saved meaning Arnor Gudjohnsen could now take the shoot-out to sudden death. Gudjohnsen, father of Eidur would later play for Spurs, saw his kick saved by Parkes and the subsequent celebrations around the stadium went on well into the night.

1985
FINALLY WINNING
AT ANFIELD

FACT **68**

On 16th March 1985 Spurs finally won an away game against Liverpool, ended a run that stretched back to before the First World War.

After beating Liverpool 2-1 at Anfield on 16th March 1912, Tottenham went 43 league and cup games without a win there. However there were now high hopes that Spurs could finally end this hoodoo on this 73rd anniversary of their last win as they were second in the league, six points ahead of Liverpool who were fifth.

The first half was evenly matched with both sides creating plenty of chances. Ray Clemence saved well from Kenny Dalglish and Ian Rush, while Bruce Grobbelaar denied Mark Falco and Garth Crooks. In the 65th minute substitute Mike Hazard's volley from the edge of the area beat Grobbelaar and hit the post but Crooks was on hand to smash the rebound into the Kop goal.

Spurs limited Liverpool to just one real chance before the end but Clemence turned Phil Neal's shot round the post. When the final whistle went their players celebrated wildly in front of their travelling fans, the win meaning only goal difference separated them from top of the table Everton. Eventually though they would have to settle for a third place finish.

1986
PLEAT APPOINTED
INSTEAD OF ALEX FERGUSON

The course of football history might have been very different if Sir Alex Ferguson had accepted an invitation to manage Tottenham in 1986.

Ferguson was attracting the attention of English clubs after breaking the domination of Celtic and Rangers in Scotland. He had led Aberdeen to three league titles, three Scottish FA Cups and the European Cup Winners Cup.

When Keith Burkinshaw left the club in 1984 the board again promoted from within and appointed reserves manager Peter Shreeves. He finished an impressive third in his first season but was sacked at the end of 1985-86 after Spurs fell to tenth.

Ferguson was in the frame and was also linked with the managerial vacancy at Arsenal, but he chose to stay at Aberdeen.

Tottenham turned instead to David Pleat, whose Luton Town side had punched above their weight since being promoted to the 1st Division in 1982. In 1986-87 Spurs played some of their best ever football, with Clive Allen scoring 49 goals as they finished third in the league, reached the FA Cup final and semi-final of the League Cup.

Pleat was sacked in October 1987 when his position became untenable due to disclosures about his private life. By then, Ferguson had finally been tempted south and was in charge at Manchester United, where he stayed until 2013.

CLIVE ALLEN'S
49 GOALS

FACT 70

Tottenham's record goalscorer in a single season was Clive Allen, who hit an incredible 49 goals in 1986-87.

The son of 1960s player Les, Allen joined in 1984 from Queens Park Rangers. His first two seasons were blighted by injury, but he still had an impressive strike rate, averaging a goal in every other game he played.

During 1986-87 Allen retained his fitness and his prolific scoring rate was helped by being a lone striker supported by five midfielders. In the opening game he hit a hat-trick in a 3-0 victory at Aston Villa and got another when Norwich were beaten 5-0 at White Hart Lane in April.

Allen hit two goals in eight more league games and his final 1st Division tally was 33, helping Tottenham to third place. He was just as dangerous in the cups as Spurs chased glory on three fronts. In the FA Cup he scored three on the road to Wembley but despite getting on the scoresheet in the final, Spurs were beaten 3-2 by Coventry.

In the League Cup Allen scored in every single game as Spurs reached the semi-finals. His tally was twelve in nine games, including a quarter-final hat-trick over West Ham. His final total of 49 in all competitions has not been bettered since by a top flight player in England.

1987
'EL TEL' ARRIVES

There was excitement at Tottenham in the autumn of 1987 when Terry Venables was appointed manager after a successful spell in Spain.

A member of Tottenham's 1967 FA Cup winning side, Venables managed Crystal Palace and Queens Park Rangers before being appointed by Barcelona in 1984. In three years at the Nou Camp he won the league title, the cup and reached a European Cup final, being beaten on penalties.

Dubbed El Tel by the press, Venables was dismissed by Barcelona in September 1987 after a poor start to the league campaign. He was then lined up to take over at Spurs after David Pleat was sacked.

Venables' first game in charge at home to Liverpool on 28th November 1987 attracted a huge crowd of 47,362. This was 10,000 more than had turned out for the North London derby the previous month, but his arrival couldn't stop Liverpool winning 2-0 and extending their unbeaten start to the season.

Tottenham were an attractive side to watch under Venables and he attracted some big names to the club. They finished third in 1990 and won the FA Cup in 1991, after which he moved up to a chief executive role. He left the club in 1993 after a fallout with chairman Alan Sugar and later managed England.

1988
GAZZA

In the summer of 1988 Spurs broke the British transfer record to sign arguably the most gifted footballer of his generation.

Tottenham paid Newcastle £2.2 million for 21 year old midfielder Paul Gascoigne. He immediately endeared himself to the fans on his debut against Arsenal, rounding the keeper to score with his stockinged feet after losing a boot. Spurs finished sixth that season and he also made his England debut against Denmark.

In 1989-90 Spurs finished third with Gascoigne providing striker Gary Lineker with plenty of ammunition. In the World Cup 'Gazza' became a national hero as England reached the semi-final, losing on penalties to West Germany.

Off the pitch Gascoigne media reported that he ate and drank too and portrayed him as a clown. To Spurs fans though he was the complete midfielder, totally dominating the middle of the park.

One of Gascoigne's finest performances came in the 1991 FA Cup semi-final. He scored arguably the greatest ever free kick at Wembley in a 3-1 victory over Arsenal. Spurs went on to win the cup, but Gascoigne left the field early in the final with damaged knee ligaments.

On returning to fitness he joined Lazio but never quite hit the heights he did at Spurs, where he is remembered with genuine admiration.

1989
WADDLE OUT
LINEKER IN

When Spurs received a huge transfer fee for Chris Waddle in the summer of 1989 they wasted no time in bringing another massive talent to White Hart Lane.

Waddle had spent four years at the club, scoring 38 goals from 133 games in the league and creating countless more from the wing. He had become an England regular and even had a single in the pop charts, duetting with teammate Glenn Hoddle to record 'Diamond Lights'.

On 1st July 1989 Waddle joined French club Marseille. The transfer fee of £4.5 million was the third highest in world football at the time and just too much to turn down.

Tottenham though invested the money wisely, spending £1.1 million to bring in Gary Lineker from Barcelona. The England striker had been signed for them by Terry Venables and scored 42 goals in 103 La Liga games over three years.

Lineker adapted back to English football immediately and was the 1st Division's top scorer with 21 goals. The following season he helped Spurs to the FA Cup and was the league's second highest scorer in 1991-92. That summer he left england to play for Grampus 8 in Japan, his final Spurs goal tally being eighty in 138 appearances.

1991
A RECORD
EIGHTH FA CUP

Tottenham's record eighth FA Cup triumph was marred by a serious injury to Paul Gascoigne in the final.

Spurs' run to the final was overshadowed by financial problems. It was generally accepted that Gascoigne, whose stunning free kick set Spurs on their way to victory over Arsenal in the semi-final, would be sold to help balance the books.

After fifteen minutes of the final Gascoigne lunged at Gary Charles and gave away a free kick on the edge of the area. Stuart Pearce scored and Gascoigne then had to be carried off as he couldn't put any weight on one leg. Gary Lineker then had a goal disallowed for offside and had a penalty saved by Mark Crossley. However ten minutes after the break Nayim set up Paul Stewart who equalised with a low drive.

There were no further goals in the ninety minutes and early in extra time Spurs got a winner after an unfortunate own goal by Des Walker. The Forest defender diverted the ball past his own keeper when attempting to clear Stewart's flick on from a corner. Tottenham's players with the cup later visited Gascoigne in hospital. He would be out for a year with cruciate ligament damage but Lazio still agreed to pay £5.5 million to take him to Italy.

1992
JOINT HEAD COACHES
FOR THE PREMIER LEAGUE

The formation of the Premier League in 1992 also saw a new managerial system with Spurs appointing joint head coaches.

The Premier League was formed by clubs previously in the 1st Division, who now took full control of voting rights and television revenues rather than spread them through the four divisions.

The other change in administration at White Hart Lane that summer saw Peter Shreeves sacked as manager after finishing fifteenth in 1991-92. Terry Venables remained as chief executive. He appointed reserve team manager Doug Livermore and former keeper Ray Clemence, now on the coaching staff, as joint head coaches.

There were three major new arrivals; a club record fee of £2.1 million was paid for striker Teddy Sheringham who joined along with defender Neil Ruddock and winger Darren Anderton. After a shaky start with no wins in the first five games, Spurs improved and finished eighth with Sheringham the Premier League's leading scorer. There was FA Cup heartbreak though as they lost 1-0 to Arsenal in the semi-final.

Despite the on pitch progress the joint managerial approach lasted just one season. Former playing hero Osvaldo Ardiles returned to the club for 1993-94, having guided West Bromwich Albion to promotion from the third tier.

On 7th February 1993 Spurs enjoyed a remarkable comeback when they scored four goals in just five second half minutes against Southampton.

At half time spurs were trailing the Saints 1-0 thanks to a goal by Iain Dowie. However Teddy Sheringham equalised with a header from the edge of the six yard box after 54 minutes. Two minutes later Nayim mis-hit a volley but it landed nicely at the feet of Nick Barmby who scored from the left hand corner of the six yard box.

After 57 minutes Southampton's defence failed to clear a cross and Darren Anderton fired in a third, then after 59 minutes Sheringham drilled the ball past Tim Flowers from the edge of the area.

The four goals had come within a space of just four minutes and 44 seconds to leave Southampton shellshocked. Soon afterwards Francis Benali received a straight red card for a serious high challenge that caught Nayim in the face. Despite their numerical advantage Spurs couldn't score again and Southampton pulled one back in the 66th minute.

The attendance at the game was the lowest of the season at just 20,098 but those who stayed away turned out in force for the next game when champions Leeds were beaten 4-0 before a much improved gate of 32,040.

1994
JÜRGEN
KLINSMANN

In July 1994 Spurs sensationally signed Germany's 1990 World Cup winning forward Jürgen Klinsmann.

The £2 million transfer from Monaco was such a shock due to Spurs facing a relegation fight after being docked twelve points due to financial irregularities that occurred during the 1980s.

Klinsmann also had to overcome an anti-German media who said he went down in the box too easily. He responded in brilliant fashion, diving on the pitch to celebrate his goal in the opening day 4-3 win at Sheffield Wednesday.

Klinsmann regularly spoke to the media, remained down to earth and kept a sense of humour. This and his performances on the pitch made it impossible to dislike him. He scored thirty goals in all competitions and was voted player of the year by the football writers.

The points deduction was overturned mid season and Spurs finished seventh. In the FA Cup, Klinsmann, scored a stunning late goal at Anfield to knock Liverpool out of the FA Cup in the sixth round. His total tally was thirty in all competitions.

At the end of the season Klinsmann left when the lure of a return to Germany with Bayern Munich was too much to resist. However he was back in 1998 on loan, scoring nine goals in fifteen games to help Spurs avoid relegation.

Spurs' record defeat in a competitive fixture was an 8-0 loss against Cologne in 1995, when youngsters were preferred to regular first teamers.

That summer Tottenham were one of three English teams told by the Football Association to take part in the Intertoto Cup, which offered the winners a wild card entry into the UEFA Cup. Although they weren't happy at the prospect, they had finished seventh in the league and were threatened with a ban from European competition if they didn't compete.

The tournament started in June and was so low key that home games were played at Brighton & Hove Albion's Goldstone Ground. Spurs lost two of their opening three group games and no matter what happened in their final game away to Cologne, there was no chance of qualification to the latter stages.

Such was the disregard shown for the competition by manager Gerry Francis, he took a senior squad to play a friendly in Gothenburg while assistant Chris Hughton oversaw a young side for the game in Cologne.

Although Spurs were not treating the competition with any seriousness the same could not be said of the opposition. Cologne had German international Bruno Labbadia in their side and he scored a hat trick in their 8-0 win, which now goes down as Spurs' record defeat.

1997
CHRISTIAN GROSS
TAKES THE TUBE

When Tottenham appointed a new manager in 1997 he was so unknown he was able to take the 'Tube' to his first press conference.

After a poor start to the 1997-98 season Gerry Francis was sacked and his replacement was Christian Gross, who had guided Grasshoppers to two titles in Switzerland.

On the day of his unveiling to the press on 20th November, Gross took the London Underground from Heathrow airport to White Hart Lane, producing his ticket in the press conference. He announced to the gathered journalists that he had wanted to travel to the stadium in the same way the fans did and he hoped this was a 'ticket to dreams'.

Gross's Tottenham career didn't get off to a good start, with Spurs losing 1-0 at home to Crystal Palace. In their next game they won at Everton but then lost 6-1 at home to Chelsea and 4-0 at Coventry. They eventually finished fourteenth, four points clear of relegation.

After two defeats in the opening three games of 1998-99 Gross was sacked, with chairman Alan Sugar blaming the media for destroying his reputation from the beginning. He returned to Switzerland, where he enjoyed a successful ten years with Basel.

1998
GARY MABBUTT
RETIRES

One of Tottenham's loyalist servants said farewell to the club on the final day of the 1997-98 season, following an odds defying career.

Gary Mabbutt joined Spurs from Bristol Rovers in 1982. He soon enjoyed UEFA Cup success and formed a solid defensive partnership with Richard Gough later that decade. A model professional, he captained the club to FA Cup triumph in 1991.

The fact that Mabbutt made it as a professional footballer at all was remarkable as he suffered from diabetes, meaning he could easily get thirsty and run out of energy. He has continued to raise awareness about the condition during and after his career.

In total he had played 581 times for Spurs and it would have been more had he not broken his leg on the first day of the 1996-97 season. His last appearance was against Southampton on 10th May 1998, when Jürgen Klinsmann also said goodbye to Tottenham. Before kickoff Mabbutt was presented with a silver salver by chairman Alan Sugar and he came on as a substitute with ten minutes remaining to a standing ovation.

Mabbutt was given the captain's armband by Sol Campbell and the crowd cheered his every touch. After the game he was given plenty of applause during the lap of honour, which many Southampton fans stayed behind for too.

After Christian Gross was dismissed eyebrows were raised when Tottenham appointed former Arsenal boss George Graham as manager.

Graham had been a player at Arsenal and as manager won league titles in 1989 and 1991. He was sacked in 1995 after it was discovered he had received illegal payment from an agent.

After serving a one year ban Graham took the manager's job at Leeds but was persuaded to leave there and replace Gross at Tottenham in October 1998. He steadied things somewhat and Spurs finished eleventh in the table. There was success in the cups too as they won the League Cup, their first trophy in eight years and reached the FA Cup semi-final.

The following season Tottenham finished tenth in the league but didn't make it past the second stage of any of the three cup competitions in which they were involved. In 2000-01 Tottenham progressed to the semi-finals of the FA Cup and were drawn against Arsenal. It was somewhat surprising then when it was announced by the club that Graham had been sacked.

The club's vice-chairman explained that Graham's position at the club had become untenable after he gave confidential information to journalists about Tottenham's financial situation. Director of Football David Pleat then took temporary charge of team affairs whilst the club searched for a replacement.

Tottenham's last trophy of the 20th Century was not won in the most exciting of fashion, Allan Nielsen's injury time header settling a dull League Cup final.

Spurs had knocked out Liverpool and Manchester United on their way to the final where their opponents were Leicester City, winners two years earlier.

Leicester set out to frustrate Spurs and rarely showed any attacking capability themselves. After an hour Justin Edinburgh was harshly sent off following a skirmish with Robbie Savage, but even then Leicester didn't do much to make their numerical advantage count. Savage himself was getting wound up and with extra time looming, he was substituted because he was in danger of doing something to get sent off.

In the first minute of injury time Spurs launched one last attack on the right flank when Les Ferdinand played the ball out to Steffen Iversen. His cross-shot was saved by Kasey Keller, but only into the path of Nielsen who headed the ball into the net.

There was no way back to Leicester now, whose manager Martin O'Neill had admitted beforehand were the underdogs. The game hadn't been a memorable one but it was a trophy all the same and took Tottenham back into Europe.

2000
THE FASTEST
PREMIER LEAGUE GOAL

83

The fastest goal scored in the Premier League was by Tottenham's Ledley King on 9th December 2000.

Spurs travelled to Bradford looking to end a run of seven successive away defeats. Straight from the kick-off a long ball was launched deep into the opposition half and the headed clearance fell at the feet of King, who was about 35 yards from goal.

King took a couple of touches to take the ball forward before hitting a low drive that took a wicked deflection, wrong footed the Bradford keeper and bounced into the goal.

It was the twenty year old's first goal for the club and there were just 9.9 seconds on the clock. The goal was the fastest in Premier League history, shaving four seconds off the previous record.

Although Spurs ended their losing streak in this game they were still disappointed with the outcome as they led 3-1 at one stage but Bradford came back to draw 3-3.

King played for Spurs for the whole of his career, scoring fifteen goals in 321 games. He retired in 2012 after being plagued by knee injuries which had prevented him from training fully for several years.

2001
GLENN HODDLE RETURNS
FOR CUP DERBY

When one of Tottenham's greatest ever players returned to the club as manager in 2001 his first game could not have been more difficult.

Glenn Hoddle was persuaded to leave Southampton for White Hart Lane in March 2001. He had rescued the Saints from what looked like certain relegation in 2000 then taken them to mid-table respectability.

Hoddle's first game back at Tottenham was an FA Cup semi-final against Arsenal at Old Trafford. Although Gary Doherty gave Spurs the lead, Arsenal hit back to win 2-1 and reach the final.

In 2001-02, Hoddle's first full season in charge at Spurs began brightly but fell away to finish ninth, below expectations. They also reached the final of the League Cup but were surprisingly beaten by Blackburn.

Tottenham began 2002-03 well and were top of the table early on but eventually finished tenth. The following season they picked up just four points from their first six games. The final straw for the board was a 3-1 home defeat to Southampton which led to his dismissal.

Since then Hoddle has had only one managerial post at Wolves, resigning in the summer of 2006 after twenty months in charge. He now runs a football academy and works in the media.

2002
THE FIRST
INDOOR FINAL

When Tottenham played Blackburn in the 2002 League Cup final in Cardiff it was the first English cup final to be played indoors.

This was the second League Cup final to be played in the Welsh capital while Wembley was being rebuilt. Due to persistent heavy rain it was decided on the morning of the game to close the roof at the Millennium Stadium, which had a capacity of 72,500. Spurs had reached the final with wins over Torquay, Tranmere, Fulham, Bolton and Chelsea. Their opponents in Cardiff were Blackburn, who were fighting relegation from the Premier League.

Matt Jansen gave Blackburn the lead after 25 minutes when he capitalised on a poor clearance by the Tottenham defence. Eight minutes later Christian Ziege equalised for Spurs, finishing with ease after some good build-up play by Les Ferdinand.

Tottenham dominated the early stages of the second half, with Gustavo Poyet hitting the angle of post and bar and having a fine drive saved by Brad Friedel. However in the 69th minute Andy Cole restored Blackburn's advantage, keeper Neil Sullivan only being able to help his shot into the net.

Blackburn keeper Brad Friedel was later named man of the match, having saved well from Ferdinand and Teddy Sheringham late on to deny Spurs an equaliser.

For the 2004-05 season Tottenham adopted a continental style management structure.

Frank Arnesen, who had enjoyed ten years as sporting director at PSV Eindhoven and was credited with discovering Ronaldo, Arjen Robben and Jaap Stam, was appointed to a similar role at Tottenham.

Team affairs were initially overseen by Jacques Santini, who had won the French championship with Lyon in 2002 then coached the national side for two years. He made a promising start but resigned for personal reasons and his assistant Martin Jol took on the role.

After losing his first two games in charge Jol then won five in succession, the best run since 1992-93. Spurs eventually finished ninth, just missing out on a UEFA Cup place. They reached the quarter-finals of both domestic cups though and there were high hopes of improvement for the following season.

Unfortunately Arnesen left the club during the close season to join the Roman Abramovich revolution at Chelsea, for which Spurs received a considerable sum in compensation. He was replaced by Damien Commolli who was there until October 2008, after which the role of sporting director was abolished at the insistence of then manager Harry Redknapp.

FACT
87

2005
THE PHANTOM
GOAL

When Spurs played Manchester United at Old Trafford on 4th January 2005, Pedro Mendes looked to have scored an amazing long range goal but inexplicably the referee didn't award it.

The score was 0-0 with a minute remaining when Pedro Mendes notices United's keeper Roy Carroll off his line. He then tried an audacious lob from just inside the United half and although Carroll got to the ball, he spilled it nearly two metres over the line and scooped it away.

Tottenham's players and fans celebrated but neither the referee or his assistant had been able to see from their positions that the ball had crossed the line. As such no goal was given even though the stadium had fallen eerily quiet and Carroll later admitted he was sure it was a goal.

After the game Tottenham manager Martin Jol said it was clearly a goal but admitted the officials may not have seen it. Referees assessor Keith Hackett could clearly see from his position in the stand though and the incident went a long way to the implementation the of goal line technology that we see in the Premier League today.

2006
CHAMPIONS LEAGUE PLACE
DENIED BY SICKNESS

In 2005-06 Tottenham looked set to qualify for the Champions League for the first time, only for a depleted side to lose the last game of the season.

Spurs were in the top four for most of the season but still needed to win at West Ham in their last game on 7th May to guarantee a place in the following season's Champions League. Tottenham's squad spent the night beforehand in a hotel in Canary Wharf, where lasagne was on the menu for dinner. Shortly after midnight, the players began to fall ill one by one.

Chairman Daniel Levy asked the Premier League for the game to be postponed but was told that failure to fulfil a fixture could lead to a points deduction. In the morning manager Martin Jol asked for just a four hour delay but the police opposed a Sunday evening kick off.

Jol just about managed to field eleven players but it was clear that most were struggling and Spurs fell behind after just ten minutes. Jermaine Defoe equalised but Spurs just didn't have the energy levels to take a grip of the game.

With ten minutes left West Ham regained their lead and Spurs misery was complete when news came through that Arsenal had won 4-2 to overhaul them.

2007
GOALKEEPER'S 80 YARD
FREE KICK GOAL

When Spurs beat Watford 3-1 on 17th March 2007 the main talking point of the game was a remarkable goal from a free kick by keeper Paul Robinson.

Jermaine Jenas gave Spurs the lead late in the first half then in the 63rd minute Robinson's moment came. After being awarded a free kick five yards outside his area the Spurs' keeper launched it forward and it drifted over the Watford defenders before bouncing over Ben Foster and into the corner of the net.

As all of Tottenham's players ran to congratulate their keeper, Foster couldn't help but let out a wry smile. Shortly afterwards he made up for his bad fortune by turning a thunderous Tom Huddlestone drive over the bar.

Hossam Ghaly wrapped up the points for Spurs five minutes from time and Darius Henderson got a last minute consolation for Watford. The win lifted Tottenham up to sixth in the table and they eventually finished fifth to qualify for the UEFA Cup.

The goal was the second of Robinson's career as he had also got one in a League Cup tie for Leeds. He left White Hart Lane at the end of the season and signed for Blackburn.

When Spurs won the League Cup in 2007-08 they became the first club to win the competition at the new Wembley Stadium.

Tottenham defeated Middlesbrough, Blackpool and Manchester City to reach the semi-finals, where they faced a North London derby with Arsenal. After a 1-1 draw at the Emirates Stadium, Spurs then thrashed the Gunners 5-1 in a memorable second leg at White Hart Lane.

The final was against holders Chelsea, who had won the last final to be played at Cardiff's Millennium Stadium the previous year.

After dominating the first half hour Spurs went behind in the 37th minute when Didier Drogba scored from a free kick. However Spurs were awarded a 68th minute penalty after a handball by Wayne Bridge, which was converted by Dimitar Berbatov.

The score remained 1-1 at full time and after just three minutes of extra time Spurs took the lead. Jermaine Jenas's free kick was punched by keeper Peter Cech straight onto the head of Jonathan Woodgate and the ball bobbled into the net. This sparked Chelsea into life but Woodgate and defensive partner Ledley King stood firm and Paul Robinson made a couple of important saves.

Tottenham's success was their first trophy for nine years and also ended Chelsea's hopes of winning a quadruple.

2008
YOUNGEST PLAYER FOR
TWO LONDON CLUBS

FACT 91

When John Bostock came on as a substitute for Tottenham Hotspur in a UEFA Cup tie in 2008, he achieved a unique distinction of becoming the youngest player to appear for two London clubs.

Bostock signed for Spurs for £700,000 in the summer of 2008 from Crystal Palace, where he had made his debut at the age of just fifteen years and

287 days. On 30th November that year he came on as a substitute with eleven minutes remaining in a UEFA Cup game against Dinamo Zagreb at White Hart Lane. Aged sixteen years and 295 days, he had broken Ally Dick's previous youngest Spurs player record by six days.

Bostock made two more substitute appearances in the UEFA Cup that season, both against Shakhtar Donetsk. However he didn't play for Tottenham again until an FA Cup tie against Cheltenham in January 2012.

That cup tie turned out to be his last appearance for the club and he saw out the rest if his contract with loan spells at Sheffield Wednesday, Swindon and Toronto. After being released in 2013, Bostock signed for Royal Antwerp of the Belgian 2nd Division.

2009
RECORD
TOP FLIGHT VICTORY

Tottenham's record victory in the top flight was a 9-1 victory against Wigan Athletic on 22nd November 2009, a game in which Jermain Defoe scored five goals in the same half.

Peter Crouch headed Tottenham ahead in the sixth minute but there were no more goals before half-time. Six minutes after the break Defoe made it 2-0 from close range then three minutes later scored another from a tight angle.

In the 57th minute Paul Scharner pulled one back for Wigan but barely sixty seconds later Defoe had restored the three goal advantage. Aaron Lennon, who was outstanding on the right wing, scored a deserved goal in the 64th minute and Defoe made it 6-1 five minutes later.

With three minutes remaining Defoe was played in by Niko Krancjar for his fifth then shortly before the ninety minutes was up David Bentley's free kick hit the post and rebounded off keeper Chris Kirkland into the net. It was 9-1 in the fourth minute of injury time when Krancjar was given too much space in the area and fired the ball into the top corner.

The win was Tottenham's biggest winning margin in the top flight. It was also only the second time since the Premier League was formed in 1992 that a team had scored nine goals in a game.

After a run of twenty league games without beating their biggest rivals Spurs finally beat Arsenal on 14th April 2010.

Tottenham's winless run in the North London derby had stretched back to 1999. When the two clubs met at White Hart Lane on this April evening it was important to both clubs with Spurs chasing Champions League qualification and Arsenal still harbouring hopes of winning the league.

With only ten minutes gone teenager Danny Rose, making his Premier League debut, opened the scoring with a stunning thirty yard volley. A minute after half-time Gareth Bale made it 2-0 when he tapped in after a Jermaine Defoe's defence splitting pass.

Arsenal threw everything at Spurs but Heurelho Gomes made three top class saves to keep them at bay. One of these was from former Spurs' defender Sol Campbell, whose header was tipped onto the bar.

Nicklas Bendtner pulled one back for Arsenal with five minutes left when he turned in a Theo Walcott cross. Tottenham's defence faced relentless pressure during four minutes of injury time but they held on for their first league victory of the Millennium over the Gunners.

Tottenham made history in the group stages of the 2010-11 Champions League when they became the first team to score two goals in every group game.

After beating Young Boys Berne in the qualifier, Spurs first game in Group A was a 2-2 draw in Germany against Werder Bremen. They then enjoyed a comfortable 4-1 home win over Dutch side Twente Enschede.

Their next game was away to Italian giants Inter Milan, where they trailed 4-0 at half-time. However in the second half they almost completed a stunning comeback as Gareth Bale scored a hat-trick, the last two goals coming in the closing stages. Had the officials awarded more than two minutes injury time, an improbable draw may well have been achieved.

In the return game against Inter at White Hart Lane Spurs won 3-1, then booked their place in the knockout stage with a 3-0 home win over Werder Bremen. In the final group game the goals still kept coming as Spurs drew 3-3 at Twente Enschede to secure top spot.

Although Tottenham had become the first team to score twice in every group game, the achievement has since been matched by Bayern Munich, Barcelona and Real Madrid.

2011
WINNING IN
THE SAN SIRO

One of Tottenham's greatest ever European results was on 15th February 2011 when they beat AC Milan in the San Siro stadium.

After progressing from the group stages of the Champions League, Tottenham were drawn against the Serie A leaders in the round of sixteen, with the first leg taking place in Milan.

It was the club's second visit to the stadium that season, having played AC Milan's city rivals Inter in the group stages. In that game Spurs were 4-0 down after 35 minutes and with that in mind manager Harry Redknapp played a much more defensive side.

Tottenham were able to frustrate Milan for the first half but in the second the home side created more chances after the disappointing Clarence Seedorf was taken off. Huerelho Gomes made two good saves from Yepe, one of them diving at full stretch to keep out a header that looked destined for the top corner.

As Milan became increasingly frustrated Spurs had more opportunities to attack and with ten minutes left Aaron Lennon broke clear and squared the ball to Peter Crouch, who slotted home to secure a famous win.

In the second leg at White Hart Lane, the two sides drew 0-0 but Tottenham's hopes of glory were dashed in the quarter-final when they were beaten by Real Madrid.

2011
TOTTENHAM'S
OLDEST PLAYER

The record for being Tottenham's oldest player is held by goalkeeper Brad Friedel, the only player to appear for the club whilst in his forties.

Friedel had already had a long and distinguished career with Galatasaray, Liverpool, Blackburn and Aston Villa before joining Tottenham in the summer of 2011, not long after his 40th birthday.

Expected to be third choice at Spurs behind Heurelho Gomes and Carlo Cudicini, Friedel began the season as number one, breaking the eighty year old record held by 39 year old Jimmy Cantrell in 1922.

Friedel went on to play all league games that season, breaking the club record each time he did. Despite the arrival of French international Hugo Lloris in the summer of 2012, Friedel remained first choice until October, when his record of 310 successive Premier League games dating back to 2004 came to an end.

Towards the end of 2012-13 Friedel signed a two year contract extension but only appeared once more in the league. This was at home to Newcastle on 10th May 2013 when he was aged 42 years 176 days. Friedel's last Spurs match in all competitions was against Benfica in the Europa League on 20th March 2014, aged 42 years and 306 days.

When manager Harry Redknapp left Tottenham in 2012, his departure showed how much expectations had risen since he took charge.

Redknapp took over in October 2008 when Spurs were bottom of the league. Three wins and a draw from his first four games in charge lifted them out of the relegation zone and they eventually finished eighth. Spurs also reached the League Cup final, losing on penalties to Manchester United.

The following season Tottenham finished fourth and qualified for the Champions League for the first time. A memorable campaign saw them reach the quarter-finals but they missed out on qualifying for the following season's competition, a fifth place league finish meaning they had to settle for the Europa League.

In 2011-12 Tottenham again finished fourth. However as Chelsea finished below them and won the Champions League they took the fourth English spot ahead of them. At one stage of the season Spurs had been ten points clear of Arsenal but a poor run of form saw the Gunners overhaul them.

Redknapp had one year left on his contract and urged the Spurs board to make a decision on his long term future. With the poor finish to the season in mind he was dismissed. His replacement was former Chelsea boss Andre Villas Boas.

2013
A WORLD RECORD
TRANSFER FEE

Early in 2013-14 Tottenham were involved in a world record transfer when Gareth Bale was sold to Real Madrid for £85 million.

Already a Welsh international, Bale joined Spurs from Southampton for £7 million as a teenager in 2007. He was a left back who struggled with injury for two seasons, meaning Benoit Assou-Ekotto remained first choice

Bale impressed in the second half of 2009-10 when Assou-Ekotto was injured and when he returned to fitness at the start of 2010-11, Harry Redknapp moved Bale forward to accommodate both players.

Redknapp's decision allowed Bale to use his pace, strength and powerful shooting to maximum effect. He came to international attention when he scored a hat-trick at Inter Milan in October 2010, a game Spurs lost 4-3. That season he won the players player of the year award and improved again in 2011-12, scoring twelve goals in all competitions.

2012-13 was an exceptional campaign for Bale who was voted player of the year both by journalists and his fellow professionals. He scored 21 league goals, winning Match of the Day's goal of the month in both January and February.

Spurs couldn't hold on to Bale any longer and on 1st September 2013 he signed for Real Madrid for a reported fee of £85.1 million, a new world record.

2015
HARRY KANE'S
30 GOALS

In 2014-15 Harry Kane became the first Tottenham player to score thirty goals in a season since Gary Lineker in 1991-92.

Kane made his debut in August 2011 in the Europa League, but his development at Spurs was not rushed. He had loan spells at four different clubs before his Premier League debut against Sunderland in April

2014, scoring in a 5-1 win.

In 2014-15 Kane didn't start a league game until Spurs faced Stoke City on 9th November. The previous week he had scored as a substitute away to Aston Villa, his first league goal of the season in six substitute appearances.

In the Europa League though Kane was unstoppable and he scored seven goals in the qualifying round and group stage. It was impossible to leave him out for league games and after that Stoke game he started every single Premier League fixture.

On 17th December Kane scored in a 2-1 victory at Swansea, beginning a remarkable run that saw him find the net seventeen times in fifteen games. The last of these was a hat-trick against Leicester.

By the end of the season he had scored 21 goals in the league, equalling the club's Premier League record. He also got seven in the Europa League and three in the League Cup, taking his final tally to 31.

Tottenham's Premier League title challenge faded towards the end of 2015-16 but they still achieved their highest position since 1990.

Spurs failed to win their first four games but three straight victories took them up to fifth by the end of September. By the end of November they were still unbeaten since the opening game, but seven draws from fourteen games meant they remained in fifth.

In December and January Tottenham won eight games out of eleven, which lifted them into second. Crucially though their one defeat in this period was a 1-0 home loss to leaders Leicester.

On 1st March 2016 Tottenham missed a golden chance to go top of the table when they lost 1-0 at West Ham. Although they won four and drew two of their next six games, Leicester won five of theirs to stretch their lead to five points with four matches to play.

Spurs suffered a major blow by only drawing 1-1 at home to West Bromwich Albion, but they were handed a lifeline when Leicester could only draw 1-1 at Manchester United on 1st May. However the following day Spurs threw away a 2-0 lead at Chelsea to end their title hopes.

Tottenham eventually finished in third place

with 71 points, ten behind champions Leicester. It was their highest finish since 1989-90.

The 100 Facts Series